Contents

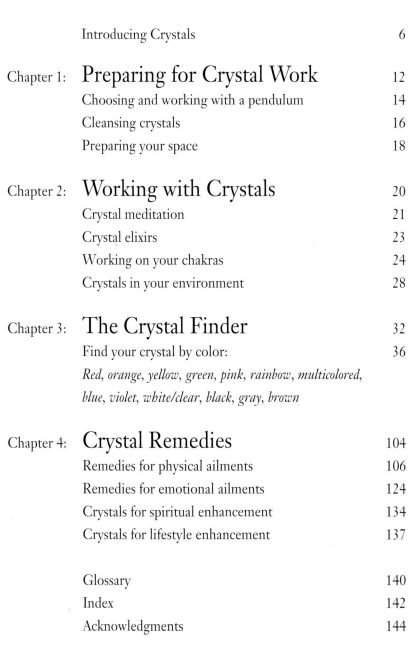

Introducing Crystals

Crystals have been worked with by medicine people and shamen around the world for thousands of years. Their recorded use dates back over 5,000 years in Chinese texts on traditional medicine, Ayurvedic texts from India, and the Bible, which has over 200 references to crystals and their powers and associations.

Crystals have been found around the world in prehistoric graves of different cultures, from the Olmec civilization in Central America to the Pharaohs of ancient Egypt. The Greek philosopher Theophrastus (372–287 BCE) wrote a text titled *Peri Lithon* (*On Stones*), which is the basis of today's modern scientific classification of gemstones. Theophrastus presented a taxonomy of known gems, their origin, physical properties, and magical and healing powers. Although the origins and physical properties still hold currency in the contemporary scientific community, the magical and healing powers of crystals have somehow been ignored.

Today, people across the world have a natural affinity for and knowledge of crystals and their healing powers. Many of my students say that crystal work "feels such a natural way of working", or they say "I feel like I have always done it". The healing properties of crystals are universal.

What are crystals?

Crystals are natural solids made from minerals. They are formed in the earth's surface. Although there are many different shapes, colors, and sizes of crystal, each type of crystal has a precise atomic arrangement.

Crystals can be identified by their color (although there may be significant variation within a crystal type), mineral composition, crystal habit, and degree of hardness. The degree of hardness of a crystal is described by Mohs Scale of Mineral Hardness. This scale is named after its developer, the German scientist Friedrich Mohs, and it indicates how hard minerals are in relation to each other.

How crystals work

There are many explanations – mystical, magical, scientific, and pseudo-scientific – for the healing effects of crystals. Until recently, everyone in the West (including me) had been trying to give physical explanations for crystal healing, but now it is understood that crystals work through the human energy system – that is the chakras (see page 24) and aura – and not through the physical body. By their influence on the energy system, crystals can effect healing within the physical body. The results of using crystals are reported throughout history and science and their healing abilities are attested to by an ever-growing bank of anecdotal evidence.

Healing benefits
Unakite can help you identify the underlying cause of an ailment, and is also associated with fertility and living in the moment.

Scientific evidence

Without crystals we'd have no rockets, guidance systems, lunar landers, Mars rovers… so really, crystal healing is rocket science! But let's keep it simple here. To date, although science has failed to prove a direct effect of crystals on any disease or condition, it has shown that crystals do indeed vibrate and they exhibit both piezoelectric and pyroelectric effects. Crystals have also been shown to hold both heat and electricity and to focus light energy. These special properties of crystals have numerous practical applications, from the use of quartz crystals in watches to the development of lasers – and crystals can even store data, seen in five-dimensional quartz crystal computer chips.

What else happens? Well, we know that crystals enhance the placebo effect (where something has a healing effect because it changes chemicals in the brain which make us *feel* better). This *always* occurs in any type of healing process, including the prescribing of pharmaceutical drugs. Finally, the explanation that crystals work by magic also has some validity, if magic is defined as "that which is beyond our understanding at this point in time".

The scientific research into the properties of crystals is ongoing. Recent research into quartz crystals has shown what crystal therapists have "always known"; that crystals increase the frequency of light passed through them. New scientific studies into dark matter and dark energy (scientific fields of study which are just being opened up), along with quantum mechanics (a branch of physics that looks at the motion and interaction of sub-atomic particles), will contribute to our understanding of how crystals work.

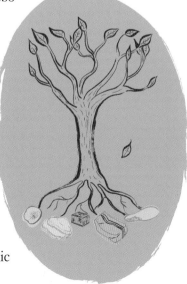

Crystals in action

This simple exercise will allow you to observe how crystals channel light energy.

1. Hold a clear quartz crystal point 2–5cm (1–2 in) from the palm of your hand. Point the crystal toward your palm.

2. Move the crystal in a small clockwise circle. You will see a point of light either directly in front of the crystal or offset to one side. As you move the crystal, this point of light moves around the palm of your hand. The clearer the crystal, the easier this will be to see.

Now try this second exercise to get a sense of crystal energy.

1. Stand with your eyes closed and your hands held out in front of you with your palms facing up.

2. Ask a friend to hold a quartz crystal 2–5cm (1–2in) away from one of your palms (the point should face your palm) and slowly rotate it. Notice how your palms feel different from one another. As we have no vocabulary to describe energy, however you choose to describe this difference is valid. Observe physical sensations such as one hand being warmer, cooler, heavier, lighter, itchier, and so on. Be aware of any feelings inside you. Sometimes these feelings may be very subtle. However you choose to describe crystal energy is fine – the description is unique to you.

Tip: try shaking your hands vigorously before you do this exercise; it seems to make it easier to sense subtle energy.

Sensing energy
When a quartz crystal is held a few inches away from your palm, you may feel the crystal's presence as a change in temperature or other altered sensation.

What is crystal healing?

Crystals channel energy. They can focus, store, transmit, and transmute this energy and it can be used for beneficial healing and energizing effects.

Speeding up natural processes

Crystal healing is about change; it involves working with crystals to improve your physical and mental health, your emotional wellbeing, and your spiritual advancement. Crystals will not do something that you (or your body) cannot, but they do speed up things that would happen anyway. For example, carnelian (see page 39) works well for common colds. Rather than curing the cold, it speeds up the symptoms. Characteristically, carnelian will appear to make your cold symptoms worse for about 12 hours as your body rapidly rids itself of the virus. After this, rather than suffering the usual three weeks of nagging dribbles, coughs and sneezes, you will simply feel better. Your body is quite capable of dealing with the cold all by itself, but carnelian speeds up the process.

Healing in old age

Now think of the healing process across the span of life: when we are young our bodies shrug off all sorts of illness; as we grow older, resisting illness becomes more of a fight; and as we pass into old age, the same diseases we once shrugged off become life threatening. The reason we become more vulnerable to disease as we grow older is because our bodies can no longer repair themselves quickly enough. Crystals help the body to speed up its ability to repair itself.

Mental, emotional and spiritual development

As well as speeding up physical healing, crystals can also speed up other processes involving mental health, emotional release, and spiritual development or awakening. All crystals will quicken these processes for you, and some crystals, particularly the ones that you are drawn to (see page 12), will accelerate your growth exponentially.

Simply sitting quietly and holding and focusing your mind on a quartz crystal for ten minutes will center you and help to still your mind. Crystals help you become open to new possibilities and this is when amazing changes start to magically happen in your life. Whether you are just starting on your journey with crystals or you are taking another step on your path, take a bold leap and enjoy the experience of change that crystals bring.

Intuitive healers
The crystals you are attracted to may reflect qualities and values you want to bring into your life. Clockwise from top: rhodochrosite (dark pink), banded fluorite (green/purple), purple fluorite, chrysocolla (blue), citrine (yellow), and rose quartz (pink).

The benefits of crystals

Crystals improve your general state of wellbeing, and reduce or even remove the symptoms of disease (often symptoms that are chronic). They also speed up changes in your life and facilitate lifestyle choices that promote health and recovery. In my experience, everyone who works with crystals sees an improvement in their quality of life. And people who follow a full course of treatment find profound change on all levels over time. Sometimes this can be a very, very short time – almost instant – and sometimes change happens over a longer period of weeks or months.

The tangible real-life benefits of crystal healing provide the evidence that it works. No doubt someone, one day, will devise a machine that can measure what crystals do, or create an experiment to prove that crystal healing exists, but until then crystals will remain magical tools that aid the healing process on all levels – physical, emotional, mental, and spiritual.

Working with The Stone People

In this book I use the term "work with" crystals rather than the term "use" crystals. The reason for this is simple – crystals are Stone People, and the more you work with a crystal, the more you get to know it in the same way you do a partner or friend. The more time you spend together the better you get on, the more you learn about each other, and the better and more effectively you work together. You don't use people; and in the same way you don't use crystals.

Perhaps as you work with crystals over time, you will realize that they really are like friends. They offer a helping hand in times of need, and joyous beautiful company in happier and healthier times. They are Stone People and, like human associates, some of them pass into and out of your life while others become life-long friends.

Familiarity
Working with crystals over a period of time means developing familiarity with them that can enhance their healing benefits.

HOW TO USE THIS BOOK

This book initially came about as a result of my 13-year personal journey with crystals, working with crystals, customers, clients, and students almost every single day. Some of the information comes from these clients, classes, and students directly. There is also information gained from research of ancient and contemporary writings. Where this has been used I have, where possible, tested the information on either myself or on my willing students. Here's how this book works.

The first two chapters explain the principles of crystal healing, examining how crystals can transmit and magnify energy. You'll see how to work with a crystal pendulum to dowse, connecting with your intuitive abilities, and understand how healers work with crystals and the body's chakras, or energy centers, to rebalance the energetic systems and bring about healing.

The Crystal Finder section offers a fantastically easy way to find out what your crystals can do for you. So often, we all have crystals that we can't identify – from jewelry we've received as gifts to little stones left lying around our homes. All we have to go on is the shape and color, and this is precisely how the Crystal Finder has been arranged. Match your crystals to the pictures and profiles, identify your stone, and discover its amazing properties to balance mind, body, and spirit.

In Crystal Remedies, look up an ailment and select the appropriate crystals for your treatment. Divided into four sections – physical ailments, emotional ailments, spiritual enhancement, and lifestyle enhancement – you will certainly find the right crystals to help, from migraines to muscle aches, colds to a confidence-boost. With full descriptions of how to work with crystals for each condition, you'll discover that crystal healing can be both satifying and simple to do.

Wherever you are on your path through life, may this book help you with each change as you walk towards health, happiness, and harmony.

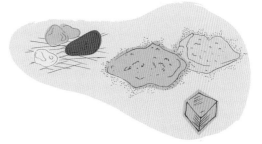

Chapter 1:
Preparing for Crystal Work

To begin to work with crystals, you'll need to choose those that are right for you. Learn to attune to their varied energies – developing your intuitive abilities through pendulum dowsing can help you gain confidence with this (see pages 14–15). Discover, here, how to cleanse your crystals and prepare your space, ready to begin healing work.

Choosing crystals

You may choose a crystal on the basis that it will help you with a specific problem or ailment (see the directory of ailments on pages 107–123), or you can choose a crystal simply on the basis that you are drawn to it.

Crystals that you are drawn to

When you look at an array of crystals there will be some that attract you. They may be pretty, sparkly or interesting, or ones you find you keep going back to. These will always help you, sometimes in strange and wonderful ways. Having selected the crystals that you are drawn to, you may discover that they were the most fitting choice in terms of how they can help you or someone close to you.

Sometimes crystals may be predictive in that they can help you with a future problem or issue. The first time I observed this I was dowsing crystals in my shop for a customer. Citrine came up for him, and I intuitively knew it was related to his digestion. He strenuously denied that there was anything wrong now, or had been in the past. I insisted, and so did he. He took the crystal. He telephoned me a few days later to say that he had unexpectedly gone out for dinner the previous night and everyone except him had got food poisoning. He had been carrying his citrine!

Whatever the purpose of the crystals you have chosen, this will be revealed to you when it is needed. I've been drawn to specific quartz crystals without knowing why. I have many of them and they will sometimes sit around for days or weeks –

or even on one occasion, two years – but their purpose has always become clear. In hindsight, each was the right crystal for something or someone very specific. So when you're attracted to a crystal, don't worry about why – just trust yourself. After you have made your choice you can discover what the crystal does by looking it up in the Crystal Finder (see pages 32–103).

Crystals for other people

If you are choosing a crystal for another person, think about that person or its purpose as you make your selection. Also, you can look at a photograph of the person, hold a personal object of theirs, repeat their name as a mantra, or write their name on a piece of paper. Be open. Crystals will choose you – they'll appear to shout, sing, dance, and jump off a shelf to get your attention.

Crystals you aren't drawn to

You may notice crystals that you don't like, yet they can also be very helpful. You don't like them because they're touching something very uncomfortable and deep inside you that you thought you'd locked away. I've seen people burst into tears or be physically repulsed by a crystal.

You may notice that you avoid certain situations in life and you don't know why. When you work with crystals you don't like, they help buried issues to surface. As a result you may cry, get angry, or otherwise release trapped emotion. This process can be rough, but stay with it – it won't last long. Afterwards you'll feel better, even transformed. You will never again have to avoid something because of trapped or buried issues. Clients and friends are drawn to you because of who you are and your energy; so don't be surprised if the same or similar crystals and issues keep coming up.

Natural magnetism
Pyrite (left) and titanium quartz (right) may be beautiful to look at, but they have unique healing abilities that you may also be subconsciously attracting.

Choosing and working with a pendulum

A pendulum can also help you to select the crystals that are right for you. You simply hold the pendulum over a crystal, ask the pendulum whether it is the right choice and then observe the pendulum's movement. This is known as dowsing, and it is a natural and ancient human ability – possibly the oldest form of divination. People have been dowsing since before recorded time. We can safely say this as the earliest writings refer to dowsing in a matter-of-fact way.

Today, dowsing is used by people in many fields. A pendulum or other dowsing tool can be used to answer any question you wish to ask; anything from whether a person is ill to whether there is a hidden source of water or oil nearby. Dowsing is used by water and oil companies throughout the world.

Crystal pendulums
Popular crystal pendulums include those made from rose quartz, amethyst (above), and clear quartz.

Dowsing equipment

You can use a pendulum, rods or a forked twig to dowse. A pendulum is the most convenient and the easiest to carry around with you. Pendulums are simply pieces of metal or crystal suspended on a chain or some string. If you are just starting to dowse, crystal pendulums are easier to work with because they magnify energy.

Choosing the right pendulum

Simply stand in front of a selection of pendulums and select the first one that you notice. Don't think too much about the choice you are making. Now ask your pendulum whether it is a good one for you to work with. (Find out below how to ask your pendulum a question.) Keep doing this until you find the pendulum that answers "yes".

Asking your pendulum a question

To use a pendulum, hold it in your hand and ask a simple question to which you know the answer is "yes". For example, if you are a woman, you could ask: "Am I a woman?". The pendulum will make a movement. Ask the opposite question and the pendulum should make a different movement. You have now identified the way in which your pendulum answers "yes" and "no", and you can ask any question you wish. To ask your pendulum which crystal is right for you, hold it over one crystal at a time and ask: "Do I need this crystal?" It's that simple.

As with all spiritual tools, pendulums respond to how they are treated. If you are serious, your pendulum will always give you the correct answer (however, be aware of how you phrase your questions). If you treat your questions as a game or you continually ask the same question over again, your pendulum will respond in an accordingly insincere way. Pendulums only work in the present and the more people's energy involved in a situation the shorter the period of time the answer will appear correct. For example, if you hold your pendulum over one crystal and ask "do I need this crystal?" the answer will be correct 100 percent of the time; you will need that crystal at that moment. If, however, you ask what you and twenty friends will do in a year's time, your pendulum will tell you what you and twenty friends intend to do in a year's time now.

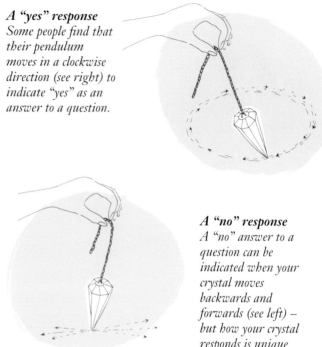

A "yes" response
Some people find that their pendulum moves in a clockwise direction (see right) to indicate "yes" as an answer to a question.

A "no" response
A "no" answer to a question can be indicated when your crystal moves backwards and forwards (see left) – but how your crystal responds is unique to you.

How do pendulums work?

Inside you is a deep inner space. Some people call it the soul or spirit, which is connected to everything. This inner space knows everything – it really does. It knows if it will rain or the sun will shine. It knows if, when you meet someone new, they are trustworthy; and it knows which crystals you need. When you ask a pendulum a question, it moves. So does your arm. But you don't consciously move it; you couldn't stop it if you tried. Watch an experienced pendulum dowser at work; their arm moves, too. This is because that very clever space inside you is telling you the answer and expressing it through the muscles in your arm. In this way, a pendulum gives you an external physical representation of your natural inner knowing.

Cleansing crystals

Crystals need to be cleansed for several reasons. When you work with crystals, either by yourself or with others, they absorb energy from you, other people, and their environments. Visibly, they can also become dusty and lackluster. You can see when your crystals need cleansing – they lose their sparkle, brightness, and even color. Crystals in need of cleansing may also feel sticky to the touch.

Geode cleansing
You can cleanse a small crystal by placing it inside a crystal geode.

Good energy versus bad energy

Crystals naturally pick up energy from the environments they live in. Any traditional crystal cleansing method, from sunlight to running water (see opposite) removes surplus energy that they have absorbed, and which is no longer needed at this moment.

We may often seek to define this absorbed energy as good or bad, but there really is no difference between the two; energy is simply energy, without judgment. Native American peoples used obisidian to fashion arrowheads just as healers recommend holding the stone to the belly to ease stomach ache. The ancient Greeks used beautiful quartz crystal globes to cauterize wounds, but leave one in direct sunlight and the same energy may burn your house down. So do not be concerned that your crystals somehow possess innate good or bad energy; they have only energy, and cleansing them helps release energy build-up, preparing them for healing work.

Removing dust

Crystals do become dusty. Dust sticks with an electrostatic charge that affects the special electricity-generating properties of crystals. Dusty crystals will not work as effectively as crystals that have been cleansed, and dust also blocks light, which reduces the quantity of photons a crystal can focus. To remove dust, lightly brush your crystals with a soft brush – a make-up brush or small paint brush is ideal. Do this regularly to avoid dust build-up.

Cleansing methods

You can cleanse your crystals by placing them in a bowl and immersing in a solution of water and a little mild detergent. Aferwards, rinse them thoroughly with water to make them sparkle. Leave your crystals to dry naturally or pat them gently with a soft cloth.

Here are some of the other traditional ways of cleansing crystals. If your crystals are water-soluble, don't use a cleansing technique that involves water.

- Running water – hold your crystal under running water for a few minutes. It may need longer if it's been working hard or hasn't been cleansed for a long time.
- Sunlight – leave your crystal in sunlight. You can also dry your crystals in the sun after washing them. Beware – quartz crystals, especially crystal balls, will focus the sun's rays and can be a fire risk. Take appropriate precautions by not leaving quartz unattended in sunlight for any length of time, and do not place on or near any flammable objects.
  - Moonlight – leave your crystal in moonlight, especially the light of a full or new moon.
  - Incense – let frankincense, sandalwood, and sage smoke waft over your crystal. You can use a smudge stick to do this (a smudge stick is a small bundle of herbs that is burnt during cleansing rituals).
- Earth – bury your crystal in the earth and leave it there for one to two weeks or moon cycles. Bury it when the moon is full and unearth it at the time of a new moon.
- Crystal cleansing – place your crystal on an amethyst bed or quartz cluster, or inside a geode.
- Sound – clear your crystal of unwanted vibrations by chanting or drumming or using Tibetan bells or cymbals (tingshaw).
- Breath or light – exposing your crystal to your breath or light is cleansing. You can also practice reiki on your crystal.

Cleansing methods
Cleansing with fresh running water (above), with smudge smoke (right), and by placing a crystal in natural sunlight (below). Do not leave quartz or crystal balls in direct sunlight for any length of time, as they can be a fire hazard.

Preparing your space

Creating the ideal space in which to work with crystals is both beneficial and fun. To make a sanctuary or sacred space in your house can help to give your crystal work a special, meaningful, or ceremonial feel. If you have a spare room or an area in a large room, your crystal space can be permanent. Otherwise you can set it up and take it down when you're finished.

Crystal placing

Take time preparing your space. Start by clearing the room or area of everything in it that you don't need, then clean the space thoroughly. Make a list of all the things that are important to you and select crystals to represent them. You will naturally find that you will need larger crystals for some things and smaller ones for others. Place the crystals about the room as you see fit – remember it's your space! Choose some relaxing music. Light some candles and sit quietly for a while in this special space that is just for you.

Crystals for your special space

Here are some ideas for crystals to put in your special space:
- **Amethyst** – this is relaxing and calming, but spiritually energizing.
- **Citrine** – this encourages fun, happiness, and joy.
- **Peridot** – this clears emotional blockages leading to a release of unwanted things and situations in your life. It's a great crystal to work with for space clearing, or to give you the impetus you need to begin clearing out old, unwanted possessions.
- **Quartz** – this brings energy into a room.
- **Rose quartz** – this allows love to flow.
- **Zincite** – this is great to display in any therapy room as it creates a healing environment.

The more you work with the same crystal to achieve a result, the better you *both* do it. It's just like learning anything – the more you practice the better you get. Some crystals do a bit of everything, while others are best at performing a specific task or meeting a particular need (like being a Jack of all trades or a brain surgeon). Both types of crystal can be very helpful at different times.

If you select a crystal and intend to work with it for a single purpose, programming that crystal can speed its effects.

Programming a crystal

Once you have chosen your crystal and identified what you want it to help you with, spend some time connecting with it. Look at it – notice its shapes, colors, and plays of light. Hold it in your hands, close your eyes and notice exactly how it feels. Become aware of its smooth, flat, sharp, and pointed parts. Take in any feelings that your crystal creates in you – these may be physical sensations in your hands or arise as more subtle feelings from deep within you. Hold your crystal very close to your ear and listen to it. Most people can hear the physical vibration of a crystal. If your crystal has no elixir warning (see page 23), then taste it with the tip of your tongue. Finally, use your sense of smell to further explore your crystal – many people can sense the difference between crystals in this way.

Connective touch
Holding a crystal in your hands is one of the simplest ways to connect with your crystal's energy.

Focus on the purpose of the crystal
Now hold your crystal in your hand and focus your mind on whatever it is you want your crystal to do. Sit quietly and imagine (or pretend – it works just as well) that the thought in your mind is going deep into your crystal. Keep doing this for 5–10 minutes.

Repeat the programming
Ideally, repeat this programming process daily for two weeks. You will find it will take you less time each day to connect to the same crystal. Ask your crystal to help you with whatever you have programmed it for. Between programming sessions you can carry your crystal with you, give it to someone to look after or leave it somewhere it won't be disturbed.

Chapter 2:
Working with Crystals

You can experience the beneficial effects of crystals simply by placing them near you, holding them in your hands, or wearing them against your skin. Try carrying a small pouch of crystals with you all the time, in your bag or pocket – they are working to benefit you during every moment. Hold or play with whichever crystals you are drawn to.

You may also like to derive the benefits of crystals by meditating upon them, as a way to help still your mind; drinking them, in the form of crystal elixirs made by immersing crystals in water (see page 23) – however, be sure to check that your chosen crystals' elixirs are safe to drink, using the Crystal Finder on pages 32–103. Discover, too, crystal healing with the body's chakras, by placing specific stones upon the seven principal chakra points.

Of course, you may simply choose to enjoy having beautiful crystals in your environment while harnessing the special energies that they bring in to your home – from helping your garden grow to selling a property, softening hard water to harmonizing all your important relationships.

Rainbow colors
From left to right: lapis lazuli, rose quartz, orange calcite, yellow calcite, green calcite, and purple fluorite.

Crystal meditation

Meditation is the art of stilling the mind. If you meditate each day with your crystals you will find that all sorts of interesting things happen. You will notice that you feel better, healthier, and emotionally stronger. You'll be more at peace, relaxed, and energized. Your mind will be calmer yet still allow you to hear yourself think. And everything you do, you will do more efficiently. Slowly, your life will change for the better.

Meditating with crystals

Begin by planning some time for yourself when you won't be disturbed. Now find a quiet space – in time, this quiet space can be inside you, but to start with it is easier to find a physical space. Switch off the telephone and any other devices that can make a noise or distract you. Put up a "do not disturb" sign to avoid others' intrusion if you need to, play some gentle music, place some crystals around you, and light a candle if you wish.

Allow yourself to breathe in a relaxed way, and feel centered. Calm yourself. Now choose a crystal to focus upon and allow yourself to explore it with all of your senses. Connect with the crystal and be aware of any sensations and feelings that arise in you: physical, emotional, mental, and spiritual. Stay with this process for a minimum of 10 minutes, but keep going for an hour if you have the time. The important thing is to repeat this meditation daily, no matter how little or how much time you have to spare.

You will find that this meditation feels different on some days to others and also varies according to which crystal you choose to work with. For example, one day you might feel relaxed yet on another occasion you might feel energized. This variation is normal. You may feel happy, calm, and peaceful or edgy, agitated, and sad. All these feelings are perfectly acceptable – go with them and don't block the unpleasant ones. They will pass.

Opening up to crystal energy

This meditation is specifically designed to open your mind, still your body, and free your spirit to be more receptive to the healing energy of crystals. Create a special space for yourself (see page 18). Surround yourself with as many crystals as possible. Sit or lie down so you will be comfortable.

So that you don't need to interrupt your meditation by referring to the following instructions, it can help to have a friend read the meditation aloud to you. You can take turns. Alternatively, you can record yourself reading the meditation and then simply play it back so you can listen without distraction.

The crystal meditation

1. Hold two quartz crystals, one in each hand. Close your eyes. Feel the energy of each crystal in your hand. Imagine this crystal energy flowing up your arms into your shoulders and chest. Allow it to fill your chest and your heart. Let it flow up into your head. When the crystal energy reaches the center of your mind it starts to see your thoughts. One by one, each thought floats towards the crystal energy and disappears into it. This happens again and again until all your thoughts have floated away.

2. Now the crystal energy drifts slowly down your body. It flows back past your chest and surrounds your heart, gently bathing your heart in clear, calm, crystal energy. From your heart this clear, calm crystal energy flows into your belly and pelvis, down your legs and into your feet and through your toes, until your whole body is filled with clear, calm crystal energy.

Crystal meditation
Holding a quartz crystal in each hand, visualize energy flowing throughout the body.

3. Allow yourself to bathe in this clear, calm crystal energy for several minutes. Just relax and enjoy it. Let it wash away any worries, discomfort, or pain you may be feeling.

4. When you feel you are ready, slowly become aware of your body. Notice how it feels. Slowly open your eyes and enjoy your space as you look around you. You are ready to continue working with your crystals, either on yourself or on someone else.

Crystal elixirs

The healing effects of crystals can be experienced by drinking water in which a crystal has been immersed – this is known as a crystal elixir. Elixirs can be effective in the treatment of certain conditions (see chapter 4); see also those crystals that should not be made into elixirs (see chapter 3).

Making an elixir

Start by cleansing the crystal you will be working with (see page 17). Place the crystal in a glass or other container of water. It is preferable to use distilled or mineral water from a pure source, but tap water will do. Cover the container and/or place it in the refrigerator and leave overnight. Throughout this process, focus your intention on what you want the elixir to do. Some people like to enhance elixirs by placing them in the light of the sun or the moon or surrounding them with quartz crystals. The next morning, the elixir will be ready. It can be drunk or applied topically over the next 24 hours. Try preparing some quick elixirs and seeing what effect they have on you. Take three different crystals, for example, quartz, amethyst, and rose quartz, and place each in its own glass of water. Also have a glass of plain water as a control. Leave the glasses of water to stand for 20–30 minutes and then taste each one. Usually, quartz tastes fresher than the plain water, amethyst tastes noticeably metallic, and rose quartz is slightly bland.

The effects of elixirs can be surprising

Working from the inside out, elixirs are effective healers. Shattuckite elixir is a general tonic for the body and is helpful in the treatment of most minor illnesses. Amber elixir is one of the gentlest, most effective remedies for constipation and after a hard day, drinking an aragonite elixir can soothe aching muscles. Some are applied topically directly to the affected external area of the body. For example, an amber elixir can act as an antiseptic for cuts and grazes or you can soak your feet in a warmed marcasite elixir to treat corns.

Elixir benefits
Crystal elixirs are simply prepared, as portable as a bottle of water, and a powerful addition to the crystal healer's tool box. Below: rainbow fluorite.

Shattuckite
Shattuckite elixir promotes general good health.

Working on your chakras

As well as the physical body we also have a subtle body that consists of channels of energy (known as meridians or nadis). When the flow of energy through these channels slows down or gets blocked, we become ill. When energy flows freely, we live in a state of physical, mental, emotional, and spiritual health. A huge range of therapies, from acupuncture to reiki, heal people through enhancing the free flow of energy through the subtle body. Crystal healing works on the subtle body too; in particular on the chakras.

What is a chakra?

"Chakra" is a Sanskrit word that means "wheel". Where two or more channels of energy cross in the body, a chakra exists. Chakras are energy centers and are the easiest places to exchange energy with the outside world. To people who can see energy, the chakras appear as balls or as wheels – hence their name.

Chakra crystals
Each of the seven major chakras, or energy vortexes, has an associated crystal that relates to that chakra's color (see page 26).

Most Eastern traditions describe seven major chakras that are positioned along the midline of the body from the base of the spine to the crown of the head. Each chakra correlates to a part of the body; an organ or a gland. As well as the seven major chakras, there are also many minor chakras (some people say up to 440), but it is fine to focus on the seven major ones.

Chakras go in and out of balance and alignment – this happens naturally all the time. A healthy chakra is flexible, vibrating, and moving slightly in and out of balance. However, sometimes chakras go so far out of balance and alignment that they take a long time to come back, and this is when a chakra needs to be healed.

Finding the chakras

It's easy to locate your chakras because they will feel different to the rest of your body. Place one or both hands on the site of each chakra (see the illustration below) and focus your mind. Notice any areas that feel different. This could mean hot, cold or tingly. You may have a feeling that resembles pins and needles, or experience an odd sensation (it doesn't matter how you describe the feeling of energy – there is no right or wrong). Energy can be felt on both the front or back of the body. You can also find the chakras on another person using a pendulum (see pages 14–15).

LOCATING THE SEVEN MAJOR CHAKRAS

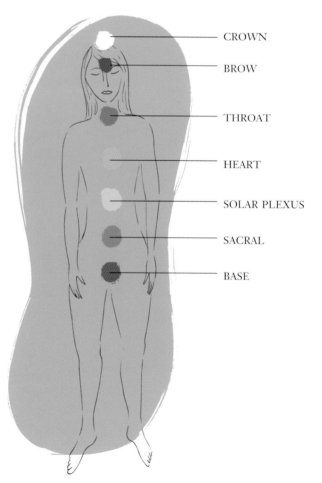

Crown chakra – on the top of the head.

Brow chakra (also known as the third eye chakra) – in the center of forehead, above the eyebrows.

Throat chakra – in the center of the throat.

Heart chakra – in the center of the chest.

Solar plexus chakra – behind the soft cartilage at the bottom of the breast bone.

Sacral chakra – just below your belly button. Try placing your thumb on your belly button with your palm on your belly – your sacral chakra will be under the palm of your hand.

Base chakra – at the coccyx at the base of the spine.

CROWN

BROW

THROAT

HEART

SOLAR PLEXUS

SACRAL

BASE

CRYSTALS FOR THE SEVEN CHAKRAS

Each chakra enhances specific qualities on physical, mental, emotional, and spiritual levels. When all the chakras are balanced and aligned many positive benefits can be felt. The chakras are associated with these concepts.

You can place crystals directly on or around the chakra points to facilitate healing. You can also place crystals on specific areas of pain and discomfort. Crystals help to focus energy directly to the body so that it reaches the areas where it is most needed. Using crystals on the chakras can both prevent and heal dis-ease.

Chakra	Association	Crystal
Base chakra	Survival, health, abundance, connection to the Earth, and moving forward in life.	Red jasper
Sacral chakra	Connection to other people, creativity, and energy storage.	Carnelian
Solar plexus chakra	Personal power, emotional control, physical center.	Citrine
Heart chakra	Safety, trust, risk-taking, and love.	Malachite
Throat chakra	Communication.	Blue lace agate
Brow chakra	Mind, ideas, thoughts, dreams, psychic abilities.	Lapis lazuli
Crown chakra	Spirituality, connection, imagination, and awareness.	Amethyst

How to place crystals

Create a special space (see page 18) in which you can relax and focus. Place the appropriate crystal (see left) on each chakra point and lie still, resting and relaxing for 30 minutes. Ideally, repeat this exercise daily.

Try to be aware of your responses during the healing treatment. You may notice one or some of the individual crystals, or experience an over-all feeling. Each crystal may feel hot or cold, heavy or light as if it's not even there and you may have tingles, like electrical sensations, either where the crystal is placed or in other areas of your body. You will often feel very calm and relaxed. Sometimes you can experience a feeling of heaviness as if you are rooted to the floor or bed. Accept whatever sensations or thoughts come to you.

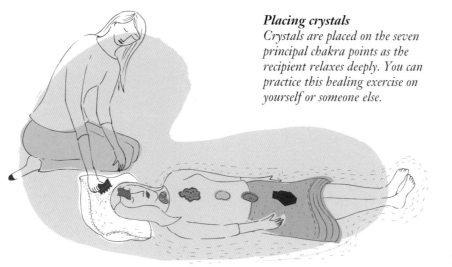

Placing crystals
Crystals are placed on the seven principal chakra points as the recipient relaxes deeply. You can practice this healing exercise on yourself or someone else.

Crystal points
Add four quartz crystals around each chakra crystal to intensify the effect.

Working with crystal points

If you want to try a more powerful version of the chakra healing exercise above, work with the crystal points technique. This involves adding four quartz crystal points, placing them on your body or the recipient's so that they point in towards the central chakra crystal (see the illustration, right). This has the effect of focusing energy into the chosen chakra, greatly empowering the healing experience.

Crystals in your environment

Crystals work whenever you're around them. You don't need to do anything to benefit from crystals that help your home and its atmosphere – simply display them at home wherever they can be seen, and at work on your desk or filing cabinets, for example, to enhance your life and sense of well-being.

The presence of crystals in an environment can also have a healing effect on your pets and houseplants. If you are treating pets with crystals, place the crystals in their water bowl or bed, or attach them to their collar with tape.

Crystal centerpieces

If you choose a large crystal you can display it as a beautiful and powerful centerpiece. This can change the energy of your whole environment in one easy go, benefiting everyone in your home or workplace.

The power of geodes

You can also place crystal geodes in your environment. They're great in living rooms or in any communal area. A geode is simply a rock with a hollow center. Crystals grow into the hollow, often resulting in beautiful structures. Common crystal geodes include amethyst, calcite, citrine, and quartz.

Said to be associated with the star sign Virgo, geodes help with:
- Astral travel, meditation, and spiritual growth
- Communication, decisions, groups, teaching
- Mathematics
- Protection for homes and changing/clearing/cleansing a room's energies.

Geodes also have the healing qualities associated with their specific crystal type (see the Crystal Finder, pages 32–103). Geodes can also heal anything placed inside them – the larger the geode, the greater the possibilities.

Crystal tips for your environment

You can place crystals in your environment to achieve anything from better relationships and communication to softer water quality. All you need do is display them safely – where they will not be disturbed, and out of the reach of babies and small children. Remember to keep crystals dust-free and cleanse regularly for best results (see pages 16–17).

For energy and balance
Amethyst and quartz crystal clusters will energize the room they're in. Everyone will feel more relaxed and at home. Place one in your living room or any communal area.

For keeping unwanted visitors at bay
Cerussite can help remove pests such as rats, mice and cockroaches. Wash affected areas with a cerussite elixir.

For work
Common opal is renowned for creating a better working environment. It's a great crystal to have around you while working in your home office and study areas, or on your desk at work.

For happy partnerships
A large piece of chrysocolla when placed in the home can help to revitalize lack-lustre relationships.

For a better atmosphere
Green fluorite constantly removes negativity from a room and cleanses the atmosphere. Display this crystal wherever you have lots of people contact, and bring it into your space after arguments or to dispel a tense atmosphere.

Amethyst energy
Displaying amethyst in your home balances the atmosphere, bringing energy but also a sense of calm.

For contentment
Moonstone creates a happy home, so place moon-stone crystals liberally around your spaces. Onyx also brings happiness to the home.

To sell your house

If you're having trouble selling your home, display a large citrine crystal, geode, or cluster in your hallway or your living room. Alternatively, you can place a small citrine crystal in each room of your home. When you do this, interest in your property, viewings, and offers suddenly increase.

Citrine for moving home
If you are having problems selling a property, display citrine to attract a buyer.

After an argument

If the atmosphere feels heavy after an argument, kunzite will allow any residual bad feelings to flow out of the room. It also works wherever there has been a death or severe illness.

For bonding

Prehnite unites people towards the same goals.

To soften water

Quartz will help to soften water in hard-water areas. Place crystals inside the water tank, or attach them to pipes. Quartz also reduces fuel consumption; attach it to the carburettor or fuel line in your car.

Sulfur to ease break-ups
Sulfur helps reduce the bitterness after a relationship has ended. Turquoise protects property.

For cleansing

Zeolites generally improve your environment, so place them in your home, office, workplace, car, or garden shed; anywhere in which you spend a lot of time. If there are unpleasant odors in a room, zeolites can reduce them – make a grid (see right) of zeolites around the area of the odor.

For break-ups

Sulfur removes negativity after arguments and is a particularly useful crystal during divorce. Crocoite and melanite are also helpful for those in the process of a divorce.

For better communication

Schalenblende helps to resolve arguments and get people who won't talk to each other communicating again. It is useful in business, improving relationships with colleagues, superiors, and others whom you come into contact with, and it's also helpful when dealing with children.

To make your plants grow

Sphene encourages the healthy development of plants, helping everything in your garden grow. Display this crystal outside near your plants, on decking, or on patios, or you can place smaller specimens in your plant pots to boost house plants indoors.

For love

Rose quartz brings love into your home, improving relationships with those who are closest to you. This crystal is also known as a beauty stone – several pieces of rose quartz added to your bath water can freshen a dull complexion, giving softer skin and a more fresh, youthful appearance.

Enhancing work and home
Schalenblende (top) aids communication; sphene (above) gets your plants growing, indoors and outdoors; and rose quartz (left) traditionally promotes love and beauty.

For peace

Display spirit quartz to bring harmony, peace, and organization to your home and to all family relationships. This is a wonderful crystal for quelling argumentative tendencies.

Crystal grids

Rather than placing your crystals randomly, you can place them in a specific pattern known as a crystal grid. The purpose of this is to alter the flow of energy towards an object, house, person, or another crystal. For example, you can arrange a grid of quartz crystal points around your bed to enhance well-being when you are in bed. If the crystals point towards your bed, they increase the energy flow to the bed. If this feels uncomfortable, you can point the crystals away from the bed to release energy.

If you are treating yourself or a friend for a particular ailment or problem (see Crystal Remedies, pages 104–139), you can arrange the crystals you are using in a grid around your body.

Chapter 3
The Crystal Finder

This chapter will help and inspire you to identify any crystals that you may already have, and to choose the crystals you want to work with to heal yourself and others (see also pages 12–13 on choosing crystals).

Many crystals come in several colors. Here, they have been arranged according to their most common colors. You can use the photographs, descriptions, and color references to help you identify different crystals. This section begins with quartz and amethyst, because they are two of the most powerful crystals used in crystal healing, before introducing reds, oranges, yellows, and so on. The healing qualities of each crystal are listed, so you can see instantly how it can help. Also included are each crystal's astrological and chakra associations, along with any alternative names. When a crystal is highlighted in bold, this means that it has a separate entry. (See also the glossary on page 140, which explains some of the terms used to describe the form these crystals take.) The common sources included for each crystal relate to those specimens you are likely to find in your local crystal store. However, there are many other sources of most minerals around the world, and local supplies may vary greatly.

Quartz

Quartz comes in many varieties and formations. It is the most abundant mineral on the earth's surface. Over 70 percent of the land we walk on is formed from quartz or other silicates in one form or another.

Quartz is the healing crystal – it will channel any type of energy and will help with all healing. If you are unsure which crystal/s to work with, try quartz.

The use of quartz is recorded in many ancient manuscripts. It heals sickness and wounds, allows communication with spirits, and exhibits scientifically verifiable properties such as the piezoelectric effect (see page 7). Cultures past and present have attributed crystals with an ability to channel light, and that light is literally the fabric of our existence – we are "beings of light". The future glimpsed through the eyes of the quantum physicist also reveals a universe made not of solid matter, but simply of photons of light.

Some of the many varieties of quartz and their healing qualities are covered individually within this chapter.

Quartz crystal

Clear or white hexagonal crystals and masses, sometimes with inclusions. (See also profiles for specific quartzes.)

Common alternate names: clear quartz, rock crystal
Common sources: Arkansas, USA, Brazil, China, Madagascar, Russia, South Africa, Tibet
Astrological associations: all
Chakras: all

Healing qualities

Quartz crystal is a "feel better" stone – it improves your quality of life, makes you feel happier and re-energizes you in all situations. It channels any energy, so helps any condition.
Physical: helps diabetes, ear infections, hearing and balance, heart health, malaise, multiple sclerosis (MS), myalgic encephalitis (ME), obesity, pain, or discomfort, spinal health, tinnitus, weight loss.
Emotional/spiritual: focuses the mind, aids meditation, and relieves negativity.

Amethyst

A variety of **quartz** found as crystals or masses. Its classic purple color is due to manganese and iron inclusions. Some rare varieties of amethyst are almost black. Other varieties are purple/white banded **chevron amethyst**, and **prasiolite**, which is a green amethyst colored by mineral inclusions.

Common sources: Brazil, Uruguay, South Africa, Madagascar, India
Astrological associations: Virgo, Capricorn, Aquarius, Pisces
Chakra: crown

Healing qualities

Amethyst magnifies the energy of other crystals. It is good for overall protection, and physical, emotional, and mental balance. It can be used to encourage chastity and relieve homesickness. It helps negotiation skills, decision-making, wealth, business success, moving forward in life, coping with responsibility and change, and public speaking. It is useful for purification during ceremonies.
Physical: heals the causes of dis-ease. Good for hearing, hormone regulation, insomnia, headaches, migraine, acne, asthma, blood clots, bacterial, and viral infections, bad posture, cancer, and arthritis (as an elixir). Good for the health of the immune, circulatory and sympathetic nervous systems, bones, heart, stomach, skin, teeth, liver, and endocrine glands. Helps with drunkenness and addictions, especially alcoholism. Aids detoxing and blood cleansing.
Emotional/spiritual: helps with obsessive compulsive disorder (OCD), and with anger and violent tendencies. Calms passion, nerves, oversensitivity, tension, emotional energy, and grief. Enhances the aura, self-esteem, meditation, spirit contact, and spirituality.

Chevron amethyst

Crystals and masses with purple and white banding in chevron pattern, possibly with rusty red/orange/yellow.

Common alternate name: banded amethyst
Common sources: India, Russia
Astrological associations: all
Chakras: crown, brow

Healing qualities

Chevron amethyst is good for general protection, and it enhances problem solving.
Physical: good for the health of the eyes, lungs, intestines, pancreas, liver, thymus, and immune system. Good for headaches, pain, infectious diseases, including human immuno-deficiency virus (HIV), and acquired immune deficiency syndrome (AIDS). Helps detoxing.
Emotional/spiritual: relieves tension. Enhances psychic abilities, shamanic journeying, and spiritual healing.

Red jasper

A variety of quartz colored red by iron oxide inclusions.

Common sources: India, Brazil
Astrological associations: Aries, Taurus
Chakra: base

Healing qualities

Together with **jet**, red jasper offers protection.
Physical: prevents illness.
Emotional/spiritual: aids rebirth, new ideas, astral travel, meditation, survival instinct, and dream recall.

Red calcite

A variety of **calcite** found in the form of masses. It is the building block of lime and marble.

Common source: Mexico
Astrological association: Cancer
Chakra: base

Healing qualities

Physical: calms physical energy. Good for attention deficit hyperactivity disorder (ADHD).
Emotional/spiritual: grounding; helps anxiety, panic attacks, and obsessive compulsive disorder (OCD).

Cinnabar

Found in the form of druses, tabular, and needle-like crystals and masses. The name is derived from an Indian or Persian word for "dragon's blood". May also be red/brown and gray.

Common sources: Australia, Europe, Japan, Mexico, Russia, USA
Astrological association: Leo
Chakra: base

Healing qualities

Cinnabar is a "merchant's stone" that enhances wealth and business and financial pursuits. Brings vitality.

Physical: good for the blood and fertility. Helps obesity.
Emotional/spiritual: enhances dignity; helps aggression.
No elixir.

Garnet

Found as dodecahedral and trapezohedral crystals and combinations, masses, and layered "plates". Colors include: red, pink **eudialyte**, pink/red **rhodolite**, green **grossularite**, emerald green **uvarovite**, black **melanite**, orange **spessartine**, red/purple **almandine,** greenish yellow **andradite**, and yellow and brown **hessonite**. For details refer to the specific crystals.

Common sources: India, Russia, USA
Astrological associations: Leo, Virgo, Capricorn, Aquarius
Chakra: heart

Healing qualities

Brings courage, creative energy, vitality, abundance, flow, change, and awareness.

Physical: helps anemia, arthritis, blood cleansing/ detox, blood flow, low blood pressure, rheumatism, under-active thyroid and deficiencies of iodine, calcium, magnesium and vitamins A, D, and E. Enhances the health of the bones, spine, heart, and lungs. Balances sex drive.

Emotional/spiritual: brings emotional balance. Helps depression, chaos, disruption, and emotional trauma. Good for magic and spiritual devotion.

Almandine

A red/purple variety of **garnet.**

Common source: India
Astrological associations:
Virgo, Scorpio
Chakras: base,
heart

Healing qualities

Almandine is helpful for people who work with numbers. Brings youthfulness.

Physical: brings physical energy. Enhances the health of the eyes, heart, liver, and pancreas. Helps blood disorders, post-operative healing, and wounds.

Emotional/spiritual: enhances connection to higher self, meditation, rejuvenation, and love. Eases death and dying process.

Mookaite

A patterned red and cream variety of **jasper.**

Common source: Australia
Astrological association: Leo
Chakra: base

Healing qualities

Good for people who are making decisions and seeking creativity and new perceptions, ideas or work. Also those who are coping with children and loneliness. Offers general protection and helps communication.

Physical: good for weight loss and the health of the stomach and thyroid gland. Helps hernia and water retention.

Emotional/spiritual: good for grounding, dreams, moving forward in life, and building self-esteem. Helps fear and depression. Aids meditation.

Spinel

Cubic and octahedral crystals and pebbles. May be colorless, red, white, blue, violet, black, green, yellow, orange, or brown.

Common sources: Brazil, Canada, China, Europe, India, Myanmar, Japan, Russia, USA
Astrological associations: Aries, Sagittarius
Chakra: base (red), other colors relate to specific chakras

Healing qualities

Enhances physical, emotional, mental and spiritual energy.

Physical: brings out beauty and encourages longevity.

Emotional/spiritual: brings out personality. Aids rebirth.

Falcon's eye/red tiger's eye

A deep pink member of the **quartz** family.

Common source:
South Africa
Astrological association:
Capricorn
Chakra: base

Healing qualities

Encourages practicality.
Physical: good for the reproductive system and sexuality. Helps sunburn.
Emotional/spiritual: good for emotional control.

Ruby

A red variety of corundum in the form of tabular crystals.

Common sources: India, Madagascar, Thailand, Myanmar
Astrological associations: Cancer, Leo, Scorpio, Sagittarius
Chakra: heart

Healing qualities

Brings health, balance, energy, wealth, abundance, knowledge, creativity, longevity, passion, and protection. Helps with decision making, new beginnings and change. Can be used for distant healing. Promotes the will to live, mental health and healing, and brain activity.
Physical: promotes a healthy menstrual cycle and the health of the immune and circulatory systems. Good for anemia, bleeding/blood loss, blood cleansing/detox, low blood pressure, and fever. Good for the health of the embryo. Protects from lightning strikes.

Emotional/spiritual: helps anguish, distress, suffering, nightmares. Good for dreams, spirit guides, astral travel, remote viewing, spiritual wisdom, meditation, peak experiences, and re-birth. Helps access akashic records (see page 134). Star ruby is good for cleansing and focusing energy, and enlightenment.

Zircon

Short square prismatic crystals – often octahedral. May be colorless, red, brown, green, gray, or yellow.

Common source: Pakistan
Astrological associations: Leo, Virgo, Sagittarius
Chakra: base

Healing qualities

Enhances relationships and personal magnetism, and brings out the best in you. Also good for encouraging purity, toughness, wisdom, and dependability.
Physical: Good for the health of the pineal gland and the bones and muscles. Helps insomnia, vertigo, allergies, sciatica, and poisoning.
Emotional/spiritual: has a calming effect and helps self-esteem and depression. Good for the aura.

Orange calcite

Bright to pale orange rock masses.

Common source: Mexico
Astrological associations:
Cancer, Leo
Chakra: sacral

Healing qualities

Brings vitality and inspiration.
Emotional/spiritual: brings calm and balances energy.
Helps with aggression and belligerence.

Carnelian

A variety of **chalcedony** in the form of orange, red, pink, or brown pebbles.

Alternate common names:
cornelian, sard
Common sources: Uruguay, Brazil, India
Astrological associations:
Taurus, Cancer, Leo
Chakra: sacral

Healing qualities

A "feel better" stone. It helps with study, memory, inspiration, speech, and the voice, and is good for live performers. It can relieve laziness and apathy and bring vitality, self-esteem, compassion, courage, and personal power. Good on meditation retreats.
Physical: reduces thirst. Good for digestion, tissue regeneration, and revitalizing the blood. Good for the gallbladder, liver, lungs, kidneys, spine, spleen, pancreas, and thyroid. Helps appetite and eating disorders, asthma, hayfever, common colds, bronchitis, infections, neuralgia, ME, lethargy, jaundice, and minor cuts and grazes.

Emotional/spiritual: enhances your connection to spirit and enables you to see the links between dis-ease and emotions so that you can deal with the emotions and prevent disease. Helps anger, envy, fear, rage, sorrow, confusion, and jealousy.

Halite

Massive or cubic salt crystals. May be clear, or single or multicolored. Colors include orange, yellow, red, blue, pink, and green.

Common sources: USA (pink and red), Germany (blue), Australia (green)
Astrological associations:
Cancer, Pisces
Chakra: sacral

Healing qualities
Good for endurance.
Physical: good for the health of the intestines and body fluids. Helps water retention.
Emotional/spiritual: helps mood swings. **No elixir**.

Spessartine

An orange variety of **garnet**. May also be red or brown.

Common sources:
China, Pakistan
Astrological association: Aquarius
Chakra: sacral

Healing qualities
Brings vitality. Good for analysis and the mind.
Physical: helps lactose intolerance.

Crocoite

Prismatic orange crystals, masses, and aggregates.

Common source:
Australia
Astrological association: Aries
Chakra: sacral

Healing qualities
Good for intuition, creativity, and sexuality.
Physical: good for the reproductive system.
Emotional/spiritual: good for the emotions and for coping with distressing changes, especially big ones, such as death and divorce. Known as the "divorce stone". **No elixir.**

Sunstone

A type of oligoclase, which is a variety of the feldspar mineral plagioclase. Goethite and hematite are common inclusions, which give a sparkly appearance.

Common source: India
Astrological associations: Leo, Libra
Chakra: Crown

Healing qualities
Brings vitality, abundance and longevity.
Physical: brings strength and energy. Good for the health of the throat, cartilage, feet, and spine. Helps ulcers, poisoning, rheumatism, aching feet, and body odor.
Emotional/spiritual: helps with fear and stress. Offers protection from "evil spirits".

Vanadinite

Barrel-shaped and hollow prismatic crystals and masses.

Common source: Morocco
Astrological association: Virgo
Chakra: sacral

Healing qualities
Helps thinking processes and reaching goals. Good for spendaholics.
Physical: good for the health of the lungs and bladder. Helps exhaustion, asthma, and breathing/breath control.
Emotional/spiritual: good for meditation. **No elixir.**

Wulfenite

Found as octahedral, prismatic and square tabular crystals and masses. Colors include orange (yellow to brown), green, gray, white. May also be colorless.

Common source: USA
Astrological association: Sagittarius
Chakra: heart

Healing qualities
Brings youthfulness.
Emotional/spiritual: good for magic, spirit contact, shamanic pursuits, and seeing and dealing with your dark side. Good for accessing altered states of reality, your higher-self, twin souls/soul mates.

Yellow

Citrine

A yellow, golden, or lemon variety of **quartz**. The color is due to heat from volcanic and other earth activity.

Common source: Brazil
Astrological associations: Aries, Gemini, Leo, Libra
Chakra: solar plexus

Healing qualities

A "money stone" that brings abundance and wealth. Good for decision-making, learning, teaching, studying, creativity, awareness, writing, problem-solving, and new beginnings. Also a "feel better" stone. Helps to sell houses.
Physical: good for the digestive system and all related disorders. Also good for eyesight and the heart, kidneys, thyroid,

thymus, and liver. Helps tissue regeneration, anemia, jaundice, nausea, vomiting, and detoxing.
Emotional/spiritual: good for relationships, self esteem, aura work, and getting rid of emotional toxins. Helps anger and yin/yang balance.

Apatite

Prismatic crystals and masses in yellow, green, blue, gray, white, purple, brown, or red/brown.

Common sources: Canada, Pakistan
Astrological association: Gemini
Chakra: throat

Healing qualities

Balances all chakras and calms the throat chakra. Good for healers, teachers, communicators, trainers, journalists, writers, publishers, presenters, actors,

singers, and performers. Good for the intellect and seeing the truth. Helps aloofness and mental confusion.

Physical: good for arthritis and tissue regeneration. Suppresses appetite (if worn or carried). Focuses healing energy on where it is needed inside the body (if taken as an elixir).
Emotional/spiritual: good for psychic abilities, past-life recall and understanding, yin/yang balance, meditation, and accessing inner self. Helps negativity.

Golden ray calcite

Rhombohedral and scalenohedral crystals. Also found as masses.

Common sources: China, USA
Astrological association: Leo
Chakras: crown, solar plexus, sacral

Healing qualities

Makes good general calcite elixir. Boosts physical and mental energy, and creativity. Helps with communication, ideas and self-limiting beliefs. Good for divination.
Physical: good for the circulation and the health of the liver, gallbladder, and endocrine glands. Helps at the start of infections.

Emotional/spiritual: good for past life recall and healing visualization. Helps nerves.

Chrysoberyl

Tabular, hexagonal yellow crystals. Some show a color change to brown in artificial light. There is a green variety of chrysoberyl called **alexandrite**, and this looks red in artificial light.

Common sources: Brazil, USA
Astrological association: Leo
Chakra: sacral

Healing qualities

Helps you to see both sides of an argument, and the best in any situation. Helps to break cycles.
Physical: good for the health of the liver, pancreas, and kidneys. Helps cholesterol problems and infections. Aids understanding and coming to terms with illness.
Emotional/spiritual: brings forgiveness, peace of mind, and kindness to self. Helps personal spirituality.

Amber

Fossilized resin from prehistoric trees that may have inclusions of animal and/or plant material. Colors include yellow, orange, brown, and green (artificial).

Common sources: Baltic Sea area; Poland, Lithuania, Latvia
Astrological associations: Leo, Aquarius
Chakra: solar plexus

Healing qualities

Good for memory, intellect, and making choices. Purifies body, mind, and spirit when worn. Brings good luck and protection to warriors; and fulfilment of dreams, goals, and ideals. Symbolizes the renewal of marriage vows. Can be burnt as incense to cleanse spaces – perfect for therapy rooms.
Physical: good for detoxing and the health of the throat, heart, hormones, kidneys, and bladder. Helps acne, bacterial infection, constipation (as an elixir), post-operative healing, schizophrenia, and asthma. Can be used as an antiseptic.
Emotional/spiritual: Good for calming and yin/yang balance. Helps abuse, negativity, emotional blockages.

Copper

Metal forming free-form shapes, dendrites, plates, and rhombohedral crystals.

Common source: USA
Astrological associations: Taurus, Sagittarius
Chakra: sacral

Healing qualities

A "feel better" stone that boosts the flow of chi. Brings vitality and luck, especially with lost property.
Physical: good for sexuality, the circulation, and joints. Stimulates metabolism and aids detoxing. Helps tiredness, exhaustion, restlessness, lethargy, general malaise, infected wounds, poisoning, inflammation, bursitis, arthritis, and rheumatism.
Emotional/spiritual: good for emotional balance. Helps over-excitability.

Gold

Veins, nuggets, dendrites, grains, flakes, masses, and – rarely – octahedral, cubic and rhombododecahedral crystals. (See also **aqua aura**.)

Common sources: Australia, USA
Astrological association: Leo
Chakra: heart

Healing qualities

Brings wealth, abundance, vitality and mental balance. Helps learning and the realization of self-potential.
Physical: good for hormones and the health of the spine, skin, eyes, and nervous, digestive, circulatory, and respiratory systems. Aids detoxing. Helps autism, dyslexia, epilepsy, coordination, sties, arthritis, melanoma, pneumonia, tuberculosis, blood disorders, vascular disease, heart

disease, hypothermia, paralysis, rheumatism, tissue regeneration, multiple sclerosis (MS), vitamin and mineral deficiencies, and tissue repair.
Emotional/spiritual: helps with anger, ego, trauma, inferiority, negativity, depression, burdens, emotional stress, tension and nightmares. Brings connection to the universe and its knowledge, wisdom, and natural healing energies.

Yellow fluorite

Yellow cubic, octahedral and rhombododecahedral crystals and masses.

Common sources: China, UK
Astrological association: Leo
Chakra: sacral

Healing qualities
Good for the mind. Aids creativity, ideas, and thoughts. Good for use in groups.
Physical: good for cholesterol and the liver. Helps detoxing and weight loss.
Emotional/spiritual: good for mental trauma.

Heliodor

A yellow/golden variety of **beryl**.

Common source: Brazil
Astrological association: Leo
Chakras: solar plexus, crown

Healing qualities
Good for mental balance, communication, and protecting things when you are away from them (for example, your house, car or family).

Physical: good for the health of the liver, spleen, and pancreas.
Emotional/spiritual: brings compassion.

Yellow jasper

A yellow variety of opaque **chalcedony**.

Common source: South Africa
Astrological association: Leo
Chakra: solar plexus

Healing qualities
Good for intellectual pursuits and protecting travelers.
Physical: good for digestion. Brings energy.

Yellow opal

Yellow masses sometimes showing iridescence (fire) in various colors. The colors are created by the diffraction of light within the crystalline structure.

Common source: Madagascar
Astrological association: Cancer
Chakra: solar plexus

Healing qualities
Helps remove mental obstacles to give you a clear perspective. Assists gut feelings. Brings vitality.
Physical: helps the absorption of food.

Schalenblende

A compact variety of **sphalerite**, yellow to brown in color, often with silver gray bands of **galena** and **marcasite**.

Common sources: Poland, Germany
Astrological associations: Aquarius, Pisces
Chakra: solar plexus

Healing qualities
Good for magic, divination, protection, travel, mediumship, and new beginnings.
Physical: boosts immunity, can help AIDS.

Sulfur

Masses, nodules, and pyramidal and tabular crystals. Yellow in color.

Common source: Sicily
Astrological association: Leo
Chakra: solar plexus

Healing qualities

Good for mental balance, inspiration, and reasoning. Helps wilfulness.
Physical: helps insect bites, infection, fibrous tissue growths, painful joints, and swelling. Brings energy. Can be used as a fumigant.

Tiger's eye

A member of the **quartz** family. Tiger's eye shows chatoyancy (an optical reflectance effect) due to its fibrous asbestos structure. It is similar to, but not the same as, cat's eye. Colors include gold, yellow, brown, blue **hawk's eye**, and red **falcon's eye**.

Common source: South Africa
Astrological association: Capricorn
Chakra: solar plexus

Healing qualities

This is a "feel better" and a "go for it" stone. Good for intuition, courage, new beginnings, absent/distant healing (especially through meditation), and sharpening the mind. Assists intuitions, gut feelings, and investigations and, as such, is useful for the police, scientists, insurers, and accountants. Helps narrow mindedness. Brings wealth and yin/yang balance and right/left brain balance.
Physical: good for nocturnal vision and the entire digestive system. Helps digestion and digestive disorders including flatulence, nausea, and diverticulosis. Also is helpful for eye diseases and broken bones.
Emotional/spiritual: good for balance, calm and grounding. Helps fear, worry, depression, turmoil, inhibition, negativity, introversion. Good for people who are deliberately obstructive.

Imperial topaz

Golden prismatic crystals and alluvial pebbles.

Common sources: Brazil, USA
Astrological associations: Leo, Sagittarius, Pisces
Chakras: solar plexus, crown

Healing qualities

Good for attraction, mental energy, thoughts, and ideas.
Physical: good for hormones and the liver and gallbladder.
Emotional/spiritual: good for relaxation and meditation. Brings a universal connection to everything and a feeling of oneness.

Tsilasite

Yellow, vertically striated prismatic crystals.

Common alternate names: yellow **tourmaline**, peridot of Ceylon
Common sources: Brazil, Pakistan
Astrological association: Leo
Chakra: Solar plexus

Healing qualities

Good for invention, intellect, ideas, mind, thought, and mental energy. Useful if you have a new livelihood, business, job, or career.
Physical: good for the liver, spleen, kidneys, gallbladder, and stomach.
Emotional/spiritual: good for behavior cycles and patterns.

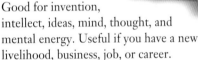

Jade

Found as masses in many colors including green, orange, brown, blue, cream, white, lavender, red, gray, and black. Types of jade include **jadeite** and **nephrite**. Note: new jade is actually **bowenite**.

Common sources:
Canada, China, Myanmar, USA
Astrological associations:
Aries, Taurus, Gemini, Libra
Chakra: heart

Healing qualities

This is a good first stone for a child. It aids problem-solving, and helps proneness to accidents and reaching dreams, goals and ideals. It brings balance, justice, modesty, courage, wisdom, compassion, and longevity.
Physical: good for the skin, hair, lymphatic system, bones, joints/hips, spleen, bladder, heart, immune system, gallbladder, kidneys, muscles, and the entire female reproductive system. Helps acne, fertility, premenstrual syndrome (PMS), menstrual problems, period pain, asthma, bacterial and viral infections, eye disorders, general malaise, high blood pressure, and schizophrenia.
Emotional/spiritual: good for emotional balance, confidence and grounding. Helps negativity. Promotes dreams and dream recall (when placed under the pillow). Brings connection to ancient civilizations and wisdom, protection, peace (both inner and outer), and shamanic access to spirit worlds.

Jadeite

A type of **jade** forming masses and rare small elongated prismatic crystals. Colors include various shades of green, purple/lavender, white, brown, red, orange, yellow, gray, and black. The colors sometimes mix and pattern or vein the rock.

Common alternate name: imperial jade (translucent emerald green)
Common sources: China, USA
Astrological association: Aries
Chakra: heart

Healing qualities

Good for magic and mending relationships. Good for use in groups.
Physical: good for the testicles. Helps high blood pressure, post-operative healing, cramps, and restless leg syndrome.

Epidote

Needle-like and prismatic crystals, occasionally terminated, masses, plates, and fibres. Various shades of green, yellow, red, gray, and black.

Common sources: Brazil, Pakistan
Astrological association: Gemini
Chakra: brow

Healing qualities

Good for perception and awareness.
Physical: good for the thyroid, brain, nervous system and skin (as an elixir). Helps dehydration, Parkinson's disease, and most other conditions.

Nebula stone

A combination of aegirine, potassium feldspar, **quartz** and **epidote**, forming smooth rounded stones with green spots.

Common source: USA
Astrological association: Scorpio
Chakra: heart

Healing qualities

Good for appreciation, intellect and freedom of thought. Brings inspiration and courage.

Physical: helps herpes, bronchitis and acquired immune deficiency syndrome (AIDS). Good for detoxing.

Emotional/spiritual: good for self-worth and seeing and interpreting auras. Good for accessing the akashic records (a collection of mystical knowledge). Helps fear and coping with tragedy.

Serpentine

Masses, fibers and layered "plates". Only found in crystal form inside other minerals. Colors include green, red, brown, black and white, sometimes with inclusions of **magnetite** which give a web-like appearance.

Common sources: UK, China
Astrological association: Gemini
Chakra: heart

Healing qualities

Good for art and creativity.

Physical: helps hypoglycemia, diabetes, parasites and calcium and magnesium deficiency,

Emotional/spiritual: good for emotions, energy flow, and meditation.

Sphene

Masses, layered "plates" and flattened wedge-shaped crystals in many colors.

Common alternate name: titanite
Common sources: Canada, Mexico, Pakistan, Russia, USA
Astrological association: Sagittarius
Chakras: all

Healing qualities

Good for astrology and astronomy.

Physical: good for physical calming and the health of the immune system, red blood cells, and teeth. Helps muscle sprains and strains, sunburn, and fever.

Actinolite

Long-bladed green or black crystals often found in or associated with other minerals. This is the crystal form of **nephrite jade**.

Common sources: Brazil, USA, Canada, Australia, Europe, Mexico, Japan
Astrological association: Scorpio
Chakra: heart

Healing qualities

Good for behavior patterns, talents, skills, and abilities. Brings connection.

Rainforest rhyolite

Quartz, feldspar and nephelite formed from volcanic activity. Flow markings may appear on surface.

Common alternate name:
green **rhyolite**
Common source:
Australia
Astrological association: Aquarius
Chakra: brow

Healing qualities
Good for choice, teaching and creative expression. Helps procrastination. Useful in any type of building work. Calms most animals.
Physical: helps diabetes, hypoglycemia, rupture, and varicose veins.
Emotional/spiritual: good for mediumship. Helps illusion.

Bloodstone

Green **jasper**, commonly with red inclusions.

Common alternate names:
heliotrope (with red inclusions), plasma (without red inclusions)
Common source: India
Astrological associations:
Aries, Libra, Pisces
Chakra: heart

Healing qualities
Brings courage, vitality, and creativity.
Physical: good for balance and getting rid of toxins. Good for the health of the heart, joints, kidneys, liver, hips, spleen, blood, and bone marrow. Helps anemia, iron deficiency, nosebleeds, hemorrhages, wounds, and blood clotting. Regulates menstrual blood flow.
Emotional/spiritual: good for emotional centering and calming. Helps stress and aggression. Heliotrope is good for controlling and releasing bad temper.

Chlorite

Often found as green phantoms in **quartz** crystals. The chlorite group includes **clinochlore** (also known as seraphinite).

Common source:
Brazil
Astrological association:
Sagittarius
Chakra: heart

Healing qualities
Physical: good for detoxing and weight loss (elixir). Good for the circulation and the absorption of vitamins A and E, calcium, iron, and magnesium. Stimulates "good bacteria". Helps chills, allergic reactions, bloating, wind pains, pain, melanoma, and liver spots.
Emotional/spiritual: good for meditation and finding answers. Helps anger, hostility, and fear.

Alexandrite

Green variety of **chrysoberyl** that looks red under artificial light. Usually small masses and, rarely, crystals.

Common sources:
Brazil, Russia
Astrological association:
Scorpio
Chakra: heart

Healing qualities
Brings good fortune, mental balance, youthfulness, and creativity.
Physical: good for the health of the spleen, testicles and pancreas. Helps nerve damage, Parkinson's disease, Alzheimer's disease, senile dementia, and leukemia.
Emotional/spiritual: good for emotional balance, self-esteem, rebirth, and accessing past lives. Helps resolve past issues.

Clinochlore

A **chlorite** mineral that forms green/white, colorless, and yellow masses, and occasionally, crystals.

Common alternate name: seraphinite
Common source: Russia
Astrological association: Taurus
Chakra: heart

Healing qualities

Good for relationships and nurturing.
Physical: stabilizes critical conditions.
Emotional/spiritual: good for spiritual love and connection with angels and guardians. Helps a broken heart and fear of the unknown.

Fuchsite

A variety of mica with chromium inclusions that give a green color. Forms layers, masses, and occasional tabular crystals.

Common source: Brazil
Astrological association: Aquarius
Chakra: heart

Healing qualities

Good for making right choices.
Physical: good for the health of the heart, spine, and muscles. Helps carpal tunnel syndrome and skin conditions, especially eczema. Aids physical recovery.
Emotional/spiritual: good for calming. Helps unrequited love and emotional recovery. **No elixir.**

Idocrase

Masses and short prismatic crystals. Colors include green, yellow, red, blue, brown, pink and white.

Common alternate name: vesuvianite
Common source: Italy
Astrological associations: Sagittarius, Capricorn
Chakra: heart

Healing qualities

Good for protection, courage, awareness of danger, co-operation, invention, discovery, and mental balance.
Physical: good for sense of smell, tooth enamel and absorption of nutrients. Helps skin rupture (for example, from eczema) and diverticulosis.
Emotional/spiritual: good for empathy and clairsentience. Helps with spiritual path, anger, depression, and fear.

Aventurine

Quartz variety with inclusions of mica giving a speckled or sparkly effect. Usually green; other colors include blue, white, red/peach, and brown.

Common sources: Brazil, India
Astrological association: Aries
Chakra: heart

Healing qualities

Good for creativity, motivation, leadership, decisions, speed and fast reactions. Helps pre-exam and exam stress, and yin/yang balance.
Physical: good for the muscles, lungs, heart, adrenal glands, and urogenital system.
Emotional/spiritual: protects, calms and soothes emotions. Aids relaxation. Facilitates contact with spirit guides. Prevents "energy vampires" sapping energy.

Orbicular jasper

A green, brown and cream variety of opaque **chalcedony**. Characterized by small circular patterns.

Common alternate names: sea jasper, ocean jasper
Common source: Madagascar
Astrological association:
Capricorn
Chakra: heart

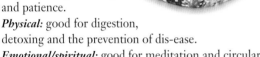

Healing qualities

Good for responsibility
and patience.
Physical: good for digestion,
detoxing and the prevention of dis-ease.
Emotional/spiritual: good for meditation and circular breathing. Helps emotional stress.

Malachite

Crystalline aggregates, druses, botryoidal structures, and clusters of radiating fibrous crystals. Green in color, often with various shades of green and black bands. Single prismatic crystals are rare. More common are malachite pseudomorphs of **azurite,** which produce a more tabby crystal.

Common sources: Democratic
Republic of Congo, USA
Astrological associations:
Scorpio, Capricorn
Chakra: Heart

Healing qualities

Good for endurance.
Physical: good for physical balance, eyesight and detoxing at a cellular level. Good for the health of the pancreas, pituitary gland, blood, heart, spleen, teeth, and immune system. Eases birth and encourages restful sleep. Has antiseptic qualities. Helps asthma, arthritis, inflammation, swelling, tissue regeneration, broken bones, torn muscles, epilepsy, insomnia, rheumatism, cholera, and tumors.
Emotional/spiritual: brings calm and emotional balance. Good for dream interpretation and meditation. Helps depression and manic depression.

Nephrite

A variety of **jade** with **actinolite**. Found as masses. May be green, black, cream, tan, blue, or pink.

*Common alternate
name:* greenstone
Common sources:
China, USA, Canada
Astrological association: Libra
Chakra: heart

Healing qualities

Good for protection.
Physical: good for general health and metabolism, the immune system, and the adrenal glands. Helps bacterial and viral infections, colic, and stress-related physical conditions.
Emotional/spiritual: good for yin/yang balance.

Unakite

A mixture of **epidote**, feldspar and **quartz**.

Common source: South Africa
Astrological association: Scorpio
Chakra: heart

Healing qualities

Good for overcoming self-imposed blocks.
Physical: encourages weight gain. Good for fertility, pregnancy, and the health of the fetus.
Emotional/spiritual: good for the emotions. Connects the base and heart chakras allowing you to move forward from your heart. Helps yin/yang balance and grief, especially for the loss of an idea/dream/goal/concept, whether or not this is associated with the loss of a loved one. Good for being in the present moment, accepting past experiences, and accessing past lives.

Chrysocolla

Occurs as layers, masses, botryoidal structures, and druses. Blue/green in color.

Common sources: Peru, USA
Astrological associations: Taurus, Gemini, Virgo,
Chakra: heart

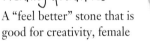

Healing qualities

A "feel better" stone that is good for creativity, female sexuality, revitalizing relationships, and for people who are loudmouthed or indiscreet. Drusy chrysocolla speeds the effects of other crystals.
Physical: good for digestion and metabolism, the hips, joints, pancreas, thyroid, muscles, and lungs. Assists the healthy development of fetus and baby. Helps breathing and oxidation of the blood, increases lung capacity. Promotes healthy insulin production and blood glucose levels. Prevents ulcers. Helps arthritis, rheumatism, period pains, premenstrual syndrome (PMS), high blood pressure, diabetes, muscle cramps, restless leg syndrome, blood disorders, such as leukemia, and lung conditions, such as asthma, bronchitis, and emphysema.
Emotional/spiritual: good for stress, phobias, tension, and guilt. Helps to heal the planet by rebalancing the Earth's natural energy. Can help to mend a broken heart.

Ajoite

Usually found as green phantoms in **quartz** crystals and, rarely, as a druse.

Common source: South Africa
Astrological association: Virgo
Chakra: heart

Healing qualities

Good for creativity, youthfulness, overcoming prejudice, and expressing your truth.
Emotional/spiritual: brings calm. Good for spirit contact. Helps self-hate, anger, jealousy, and prejudice. Replaces fear with love.

Green opal

Green masses sometimes showing iridescence (fire) in various colors. The colors are created by the diffraction of light within the crystalline structure.

Common alternate name: Andean **opal**
Common source: Peru
Astrological associations: Aries, Cancer, Sagittarius
Chakra: heart

Healing qualities

Good for awareness, problem solving, hypnosis, and divination.
Physical: good for the immune system. Helps detoxing and understanding the nutritional needs of yourself and others. Helps colds, flu, temperature balance, fever, and hypothermia.
Emotional/spiritual: good for grounding, centering, relaxing, meditating, and shamanic journeying. Good for encouraging and remembering dreams.

Amazonite

A green, usually opaque, variety of microcline (a variety of feldspar), in the form of crystals and masses. Color varies from yellow-green to blue-green.

Common alternate names: Amazon jade, Amazon stone
Common sources: Brazil, Russia, USA
Astrological association: Virgo
Chakra: heart

Healing qualities

A "feel better" stone that is good for creativity.
Physical: good for the heart, nerves, and nervous system. Helps schizophrenia.
Emotional/spiritual: soothing and calming. Good for the aura. Helps stress, nervousness, and a troubled mind.

Brazilianite

Short, striated prismatic colorless or green crystals.

Common source: Brazil
Astrological association:
Capricorn
Chakra: heart

Healing qualities

Good for desire
and relationships.
Facilitates making
and coping with
decisions.
Physical: helps fever, sunstroke, heatstroke, sensitive
skin, and sunburn.
Emotional/spiritual: gently releases trapped emotions
and energy.

Pyromorphite

Hexagonal prismatic crystals, druses, botryoidal
structures and masses in green, yellow, brown, and
orange.

Common sources: UK,
China
*Astrological
associations:* Aries,
Leo, Sagittarius
Chakra: heart

Healing qualities

Good for humor and new beginnings.
Physical: good for the health of the gums. Helps
vitamin B deficiency, chills, and gum disease.
Emotional/spiritual: brings confidence. **No elixir.**

Adamite

Yellow-green tabular crystals or druse with a vitreous
luster.

Common source: Mexico
Astrological association: Cancer
Chakra: heart

Healing qualities

Good for business success, wealth, expression, lateral
thinking, intellect and inner strength.
Physical: good for the health of the heart, lungs, throat,
and ductless glands.

Emotional/spiritual: good for the emotions generally.

Green calcite

Masses that are bright emerald to pale green in color.

Common source: Mexico
Astrological association: Cancer
Chakra: heart

Healing qualities

Physical: good for the prevention and treatment of
infection.
Emotional/spiritual: calms
emotions. Helps anxiety,
panic attacks. Enables
you to cope when
other people are
laughing at your
expense.

Emerald

A green gem variety of **beryl**.

Common sources: Columbia (for gem quality), Brazil (for commercial grade)
Astrological associations: Aries, Taurus, Gemini
Chakra: heart

Healing qualities

Brings vitality. Good for memory, patience, and honesty.

Physical: good for growth, balance, eyesight, and fertility. Good for the health of the kidneys, liver, bile ducts, bones, teeth, heart, and immune system. Helps biliousness, insect bites, high blood pressure, asthma, inflammation, jaundice, bacterial and viral infections, sores, and angina. Has antiseptic qualities.
Emotional/spiritual: helps bad temper.

Dioptase

Brilliant emerald green prismatic crystals and masses.

Common sources: Namibia, Democratic Republic of Congo, Russia, USA
Astrological associations: Scorpio, Sagittarius
Chakras: all

Healing qualities

Brings vitality, abundance, and balance. Helps change, renewing ideals, and being in the moment.
Physical: good for nutritional balance, the lungs, immune system, heart, circulation, and stomach. Good for development in babies. Aids understanding of the causes of disease. Helps blood pressure, diarrhea, nausea, irritable bowel syndrome (IBS), ulcers, Ménière's disease, dizziness,

AIDS, varicose veins, angina, and pain.
Emotional/spiritual: brings yin/yang balance, past life access, and emotional stability. Helps oppression.

Uvarovite

An emerald green variety of **garnet**.

Common source: Russia
Astrological association: Aquarius
Chakra: heart

Healing qualities

Promotes clear thinking.
Physical: good for detoxing and for the health of the heart and lungs. Helps frigidity, acidosis, leukemia, and kidney, and bladder infections.
Emotional/spiritual: calming and good for the soul. Helps alleviate loneliness. Facilitates finding twin souls/soul mates.

Prehnite

Found as massive botryoidal and globular structures, layered "plates", and tabular and prismatic crystals. Colors are green, yellow, white, and brown.

Common source: Australia
Astrological association: Libra
Chakras: heart, brow

Healing qualities

Good for divination, prophecy, visualization, inspiration, and flow.
Physical: good for the health of the connective tissue, kidneys, and bladder. Helps anemia and gout.
Emotional/spiritual: good for meditation, calmness, letting go, and finding your own true spiritual path through life. Helps agitation, dreams, and dream recall.

Wavellite

Found as masses, globe-like shapes, druses, and needle-like crystals. May be colorless, green, white, yellow, brown, black, or blue.

Common source: USA
Astrological association: Aquarius
Chakra: heart

Healing qualities
Helps intuition, choices, and decision-making. Good for energy flow.
Physical: preserves health when you are healthy. Good for bodily fluids. Helps dermatitis.

Tree agate

Opaque masses of **agate** with green and white patterns that resemble foliage.

Common source: India
Astrological association: Taurus
Chakra: heart

Healing qualities
Helps you to see the beauty in everything. Good for cultivating plants; useful for gardeners.
Emotional/spiritual: very calming. Helps shock, and trauma and matters related to the ego.

Bowenite

Fine granular green masses of antigorite.

Common alternate names: new jade, tangiwaite, tangawaite, greenstone (used in New Zealand – note that "greenstone" is also a common name for **nephrite jade**, which is a different mineral)
Common sources: China, USA
Astrological association: Aquarius
Chakra: heart

Healing qualities
Known as the "stone of the warrior" – protects you from enemies. Brings love, friendship, connection to your ancestors, success in business, and helps you meet personal goals and ambitions. Useful when moving home – helps you make a clean break from the past. Helps you remove self-imposed obstacles. Facilitates change and adventure. Useful for finding soul mates.
Physical: good for the heart, cholesterol, fertility, and DNA/RNA. Helps with acrophobia (fear of heights).
Emotional/spiritual: good for meditation. Helps with grief, depression, and past traumas.

Variscite

Found as masses, nodules, druses, and octahedral crystals. Various shades of green, and, rarely, red.

Common sources: Australia, USA
Astrological associations: Taurus, Gemini, Scorpio
Chakra: heart

Healing qualities
Good for masculine qualities. Useful for carers.
Physical: good for the health of the fetus.

Good for the nervous system, penis, testicles, prostate gland, and the elasticity of the skin. Helps abdominal distension, wind pains, blood flow, and impotency.
Emotional/spiritual: calming. Brings emotional stability. Helps despair.

Chrysoprase

Green or yellow (lemon) variety of **chalcedony**.

Common source: Australia
Astrological association: Libra
Chakra: heart

Healing qualities

A "feel better" stone.
Good for general mental
health and healing.
Helps you to see
through mental fog.
Good for dexterity.
Physical: good for fertility and the health of the spleen
and heart. Helps schizophrenia and scurvy.
Emotional/spiritual: good for yin/yang balance,
meditation, balance, self acceptance, and acceptance of
others. Helps anxiety, depression, fear, neurotic
patterns, stress, inferiority, broken heart, and
judgmental attitudes. Combats feelings of arrogance
and superiority.

Grossularite

A green variety of **garnet**. Also colorless, yellow,
brown, red-brown, red, orange, white, gray, and black.

Common alternate name: grossular garnet
Common source: Malawi
Astrological association: Cancer
Chakra: heart

Healing qualities

Good for reason.
Physical: good for fertility
(meditate with it). Helps
vitamin A deficiency.
Emotional/spiritual:
helps with
arguments and
disputes.

Zoisite

Masses and striated prismatic crystals. May be colorless,
green, brown, red, yellow, white, lavender, blue
tanzanite, and pink **thulite**.

Common sources: Pakistan, Tanzania, Zimbabwe,
Scotland
Astrological association:
Gemini
Chakra: heart

Healing qualities

Good for laziness
and idleness.
Physical: good for
the heart,
spleen, pancreas,
and lungs.
Emotional/spiritual: helps negativity.

Anyolite

Ruby crystals growing through masses of **zoisite**.

Common alternate names: **zoisite** and **ruby**
Common source: Tanzania
Astrological associations: Gemini,
Cancer, Leo, Scorpio,
Sagittarius
Chakras:
heart,
crown

Healing qualities

Good for mind and vitality.
Physical: good for the heart. Useful for diagnosis. Helps
if you are generally run down.
Emotional/spiritual: good for altered states of
consciousness, psychic abilities, and communication
with spirits.

Peridot

Small green prismatic crystals and masses. Other colors include red, brown, and yellow.

Common alternate names: chrysolite, olivine
Common sources: Afghanistan, Brazil, Canary Islands, Pakistan, Russia, Sri Lanka, USA
Astrological associations: Leo, Virgo, Scorpio, Sagittarius
Chakra: heart

Healing qualities
A "feel better" stone that is good for the ego and mental health and healing. Offers protection from outside influences. Helps with laziness and breaks behavior patterns and cycles.
Physical: good for the health of the colon, heart, lungs, spleen, pancreas, intestines, liver, and gallbladder. Helps digestion and detoxing. Acts as a general physical tonic. Stimulates contractions during labor. Helps with astigmatism, near-sightedness, sunburn, poisons, addictions, alcoholism, gastroenteritis, cancer, acidity, irritable bowel syndrome (IBS), Crohn's disease, ulcers, and weight gain.
Emotional/spiritual: good for enlightenment through meditation. Helps with stress, anger, jealousy, depression, emotional blockages, and lethargy.

Green moss agate

Transparent or translucent green, white, and clear moss-like patterned masses of **agate**. May also be red, yellow, brown, black, and blue.

Common source: India
Astrological association: Virgo
Chakra: heart

Healing qualities
Good for wealth. Helps the growth of new crops.
Physical: good for cleansing and detox. Good for digestion, the immune system and eyes. Helps dehydration, fungal infection, cold and flu symptoms, and skin disorders.
Emotional/spiritual: releases trapped emotions. Helps anxiety, stress, and tension.

Beryl

Hexagonal prismatic crystals with flat or occasionally small pyramidal terminations. Colors are milky yellow/green, green **emerald**, white, blue **aquamarine**, yellow/gold **heliodor**, red bixbite, pink **morganite**, or colorless **goshenite.**

Common sources: Africa, Brazil, Pakistan, Russia
Astrological associations: Aries, Gemini, Leo, Pisces
Chakras: crown, solar plexus

Healing qualities
Brings adaptability, activity, initiative, wisdom, and vitality. Helps you to fulfil your potential. Good for use in ceremonies. See specific varieties of beryl for other healing qualities.
Physical: good for the nervous system and pancreas. Calms belching.
Emotional/spiritual: good for emotional balance and 21st-century stress.

Green fluorite

Green cubic, octahedral, and rhombododecahedral crystals and masses.

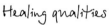

Common sources: China, UK
Astrological associations: Capricorn, Pisces
Chakra: heart

Healing qualities
Clears negativity from a room.
Physical: good for the health of the stomach, intestines, and colon. Helps colitis, heartburn, nausea, and sore throat.
Emotional/spiritual: good for cleansing the chakras. Helps mild emotional upsets.

Verdelite

A green variety of **tourmaline**.

Common sources: Brazil, Pakistan
Astrological association: Capricorn
Chakras: heart, brow

Healing qualities
Brings abundance, creativity, and success. Good for the brain, thoughts, ideas and peace of mind. Helpful for herbalists and can assist them in their work.
Physical: good for the eyes, heart, thymus, and immune system. Helps constipation and weight loss.
Emotional/spiritual: good for feelings generally. Brings compassion. Assists visualization. Helps with negativity and abuse.

Moldavite

Green **tektite** that was originally created from meteorites impacting on the earth's surface and melting themselves – and the earth – on impact. This is the resulting reformed natural glass material: part earth, part space.

Common alternate name: valtava
Common source: the *sole* source is the Czech Republic
Astrological associations: all
Chakras: brow, heart

Healing qualities
Brings mental balance. Opens the mind to new possibilities. Good for new experiences.
Physical: a soft general tonic that brings physical balance.
Emotional/spiritual: facilitates altered mind states (for example, meditation, dreams, and hypnosis). Good for clairsentience.

Prasiolite

A green variety of **amethyst** that is colored by minerals in underground water.

Common source: Brazil
Astrological associations: Scorpio, Capricorn
Chakra: heart

Healing qualities
Physical: good for understanding the cause of disease.
Emotional/spiritual: good for connection to nature, looking deeper into yourself and reaching inner depths in meditation (you may not like it, but it's good for you!). Helps you find your inner core and self. Corrects erroneous growth.

Hiddenite

A green variety of **kunzite**.

Common source: Pakistan
Astrological association: Scorpio
Chakra: brow

Healing qualities
Good for the intellect and study.
Physical: good for the lungs. Aids diagnosis.
Emotional/spiritual: aids spiritual understanding. Can be used to brush "knots" from the aura.

Pink banded agate

A variety of **agate** with pink, white, and sometimes gray banding and patterns.

Common source: Botswana
Astrological associations: Taurus, Scorpio
Chakras: heart, sacral

Healing qualities

Good for femininity, creativity, nurture, finding solutions to problems, and attention to detail. Helps you to see the whole picture.
Physical: good for the nervous system. Helps detoxing.
Emotional/spiritual: brings universal love. Helps depression and stress.

Manganoan calcite

Found as masses with pink and white bands.

Common alternate names:
mangano calcite
Common source:
Peru
Astrological association:
Cancer
Chakra: heart

Healing qualities

Physical: helps sleep.
Emotional/spiritual: brings love, peace, calm and rest. Relieves abuse, trauma, nightmares, and anxiety.

Cobaltoan calcite

Drusy crusts, spherical masses, and, rarely, crystals. Often found with or near **malachite**.

Common alternate name:
cobaltocalcite
Common sources:
Democratic Republic of Congo, Morocco
Astrological association:
Cancer
Chakras: heart, throat, brow, crown

Healing qualities

Emotional/spiritual: helps you to see the beauty in everyone and in everything, and to recognize and learn each lesson along your path in life. Helps you to discover your inner truth and life purpose. Draws out inner hurts and emotional pain. Facilitates emotional expression.

Erythrite

Pink (pale pink to purple) and gray blades, globular masses, often with a crystalline surface druse, and prismatic crystals.

Common source: Morocco
Astrological associations: Taurus, Virgo, Capricorn
Chakra: throat

Healing qualities

Good for communication and perspective.
Physical: Good for skin, bone marrow, and red blood cells.
Helps inflammation and throat infections. **No elixir.**

Eudialyte

A variety of pink **garnet** often intermingled with other minerals.

Common source: Russia
Astrological association:
Aries
Chakra: heart

Healing qualities
Physical: good for eye disorders.
Emotional/spiritual: good for emotional release, opening the heart, and connecting with childhood, the past and past lives. Brings extra-sensory perception (ESP), self love, and forgiveness. With **metamorphosis quartz**, it eases the discomfort of change.

Kunzite

A pink variety of spodumene forming flattened prismatic crystals with vertical striations. May also be clear, lilac, blue, green **hiddenite**, or yellow. Crystals may be two or three different colors.

Common source: Afghanistan
Astrological associations: Aries, Taurus, Leo, Libra, Scorpio
Chakra: heart

Healing qualities
A "feel better" stone that is good for love, expression and flow (it removes obstacles

from your path). Can remove negativity in the environment and act as a protective shield.
Physical: good for female sexuality, and the heart, blood pressure, skin, and lungs. Aids hormone secretion and brings youthful appearance. Helps with addictions, smoking cessation, premenstrual tension (PMT), and period pains. Removes energy blocks that can cause physical dis-ease.
Emotional/spiritual: brings calm. Good for self-esteem,

centering and meditation. Helps desire, control, compulsive behavior, immaturity, depression, and all stress-related conditions.

Morganite

A pink variety of **beryl**.

Common sources: Brazil, Pakistan
Astrological association: Libra
Chakra: heart

Healing qualities
Brings wisdom and clear thought. Helps you to see a different perspective. Good for time saving. Useful in ceremonies.
Physical: good for physical healing and oxygenation of blood. Helps chest conditions such as asthma, emphysema, and tuberculosis (TB).
Emotional/spiritual: brings calm. Good for love, meditation and contact with spirit guides. Fills the space left in the heart by loss through broken relationships or death. Helps racism and sexism.

Pink opal

Pink masses, sometimes showing iridescence.

Common source: Peru
Astrological association: Cancer
Chakra: heart

Healing qualities
Good for clearing the mind.
Physical: good for the lungs, spleen, heart, and connective tissue. Helps diabetes and hypoglycemia. Soothes the skin.
Emotional/spiritual: self-healing, rebirth, spiritual awakening, renewal, and love. Calming, helps behavior patterns and violent behavior.

Strawberry quartz

A pink variety of **quartz**, the color of crushed strawberries.

Common source: South Africa
Astrological association: Libra
Chakras: heart, crown

Healing qualities

Helps you to see the reality in any situation.
Emotional/spiritual: good for love. Channels away energy you are not using, leading to peace of mind, calmness, and restful sleep.

Rose quartz

Pink crystalline masses and, rarely, hexagonal crystals.

Common sources: Brazil, India, Madagascar, South Africa
Astrological associations: Taurus, Libra
Chakra: heart

Healing qualities

Magnifies creativity and imagination. Good for writing, art, and music.
Physical: good for complexion, youthful appearance, fertility and the menstrual cycle. Good for the health of the adrenal glands, heart, blood, circulation, kidneys, and spleen. Helps general aches and pains, wrinkles, asthma, vertigo, coughs, flu, varicose veins, and burns (including sunburn). Balances sex drive and helps sexual frustration. Helps detoxing.
Emotional/spiritual: calming. Good for forgiveness, love, romance and relationships. Enhances female energy and qualities. Helps crisis, phobias, anger, stress, tension, fear, guilt, grief, inadequacy, jealousy, resentment, and the feeling of being emotionally wounded. Helps childhood experiences and emotions. Like a bubble bath for the emotions.

Rhodochrosite

Found as masses, druses, botryoidal structures, and rare small rhombohedral crystals. Colors range from pale pink to deep red, yellow, orange, and brown. When rhodochrosite is tumble polished, it typically has pink and white bands.

Common source: Argentina
Astrological associations:
Leo, Scorpio
Chakra: heart

Healing qualities

Brings courage. Good for memory, passion, sex, and making music.
Physical: good for the spleen, heart, circulation, and kidneys. Helps aging and myalgic encephalomyelitis (ME). Promotes the healthy development of babies.
Emotional/spiritual: good for flow and yin/yang balance. Helps mental breakdown, 21st-century stress, and emotional trauma.

Rhodolite

A pink/red variety of **garnet**.

Common sources: Mexico, USA
Astrological association: Leo
Chakras: base, heart

Healing qualities

Good for intuition and inspiration.
Physical: good for the heart and lungs.
Emotional/spiritual: calming and good for meditation, contemplation, and channeling. Helps energy flow throughout the body. Helps to release energy blocks.

Rhodonite

Pink or red tabular crystals and masses, also found in green, yellow and black, usually with veined inclusions of manganese that produce black lines.

Common sources: Australia, Cornwall, Madagascar, South Africa, USA
Astrological association: Taurus
Chakra: heart

Healing qualities
Good for mental balance, attention to detail, memory and making music (especially together with rhodochrosite).
Physical: good for the heart and bones. Helps schizophrenia, myalgic encephalomyelitis (ME), emphysema, arthritis, light sensitivity, and throat infections.
Emotional/spiritual: calming and good for yin/yang balance, unconditional spiritual love, self-esteem, and sensitivity. Grounds the feeling of love in the physical world. Helps anxiety, mental unrest, confusion, 21st-century stress, and inconsistency.

Smithsonite

Druses, masses and botryoidal structures, and scalenohedral and rhombohedral crystals. Colors include pink, green, blue, lavender, purple, brown, yellow, and grayish white.

Common source: Namibia
Astrological associations: Virgo, Pisces
Chakra: heart

Healing qualities
Good for leadership and disputes (smoothing the waters). Brings vitality. Helps new beginnings to start.
Physical: good for digestion and the health of the veins, immune system and sinuses. Helps spots, alcoholism, and osteoporosis.

Emotional/spiritual: brings calmness, pleasantness, kindness, clairvoyance, and clairsentience.

Thulite

A pink variety of **zoisite**.

Common sources: Norway, USA
Astrological associations: Taurus, Gemini
Chakra: heart

Healing qualities
A calm and gentle stone that is good for actors. Encourages eloquence, and helps aimlessness, vanity, and conceit.
Physical: helps calcium deficiency, flatulence, and wind pains.
Emotional/spiritual: helps you find your inner self and your path in life.

Elbaite

A pink variety of **tourmaline**.

Common source: Brazil
Astrological association: Libra
Chakra: heart

Healing qualities
Good for awareness, creativity and new beginnings.
Physical: good for hormone balance and the heart, lungs, and skin. Helps infirmity.
Emotional/spiritual: good for love, including spiritual love. Helps destructive behavior and mending a broken heart.

Rainbow

Rainbow colors includes those minerals that usually exhibit several colors at once, and is followed by a selection of multicolored stones, such as agate and onyx, which come in a range of colors.

Abalone shell

The shell of a marine mollusc. Contains minerals that produce a range of brilliant colors.

Common alternate names: paua shell, sea opal (this should not be confused with opalite which is also known as sea opal but is man-made)

Common source: oceans around most continents, Australia, Japan, New Zealand, USA, Vietnam
Astrological associations: Cancer, Scorpio, Aquarius, Pisces
Chakra: throat

Healing qualities
Good for power, femininity, and seeing beauty.
Physical: good for the eyes. Aids detoxing. Helps reduce physical tension and builds physical strength. Helps cataracts and hemeralopia (inability to see in bright light).
Emotional/spiritual: good for love, relaxation, and letting go of emotions. Facilitates connection with ancestors.

Fire agate

Agate occurring as pebbles in brownish colors with flashes of "fire" due to thin layers of limonite.

Common source: Mexico
Astrological association: Aries
Chakra: brow

Healing qualities
Good for inspiration and action. Offers a shield of protection.
Physical: good for eyes, sight, and night vision.
Emotional/spiritual: good for emotional control, clairvoyance, connection to spirits, and spirituality. Helps fear.

Bornite

Found as metallic masses with copper-red flashes that oxidize in air and moisture to produce blue/green/gold/purple colors.

Common alternate names: peacock ore, peacock rock, purple copper (ore)
Common sources: Mexico
Astrological association: Cancer
Chakras: all

Healing qualities
Good for creative expression and removing self-imposed obstacles.
Physical: good for salt balance, physical energy, and the kidneys. Good for the healthy development of babies. Helps acid indigestion, epilepsy, fever, gout, swelling, anemia, and angina. Calms adrenaline.
Emotional/spiritual: good for happiness, joy, being in the moment, emotional energy, re-birthing, and left/right brain balance. Puts color back into flat energy. Helps grief and speeds karma.

Labradorite

Masses of plagioclase feldspar with albite, occasionally forming tabular crystals. May be colorless, gray-green, pale green, blue, or gray-white. The brilliant flashes of blue, red, gold, and green are due to light interference within the structure of the minerals' composition.

Common alternate names: black moonstone, Labrador moonstone, Labrador feldspar, spectrolite
Common source: Canada, Madagascar, Norway
Astrological associations: Leo, Scorpio, Sagittarius
Chakra: crown

Healing qualities
Good for mental sharpness, intellect, right/left brain activity, inspiration, intuition, and originality. Lets you see many possibilities at once. Aids scientific analysis.
Physical: good for digestion and the eyes. Helps warts (hold, rub gently, or tap the stone).
Emotional/spiritual: allows magic to happen. Stabilizes the aura and enhances the flow of energy between the aura and the chakras. Helps with insecurity, anxiety, and stress.

Rainbow obsidian

Volcanic glass, occuring in a variety of colors.

Common source: Mexico
Astrological association: Libra
Chakra: base

Healing qualities
Useful for divination and hypnosis.
Emotional/spiritual: connecting with nature, your inner self, seeing the beauty in everything, happiness, and the aura. Helps stress.

Opal

Occurs as masses in a multitude of colors including white **common**, **pink**, **black**, beige, **blue**, **yellow**, brown, orange, red, **green**, and purple, sometimes showing iridescence (fire) in various colors. Colors are produced by the diffraction of light within the crystalline structure. Common opal does not have a diffraction grating in its structure and shows no color as a result.

Common sources: Australia, Peru, USA
Astrological associations: Cancer, Libra, Scorpio, Pisces
Chakras: heart, throat, crown

Healing qualities
Good for creativity, inspiration, imagination, and memory.
Physical: good for the kidneys, eyes, vision, and circulation. Aids detox. Helps infections, diabetes, fever, Parkinson's disease, and cholera. Useful during childbirth.
Emotional/spiritual: promotes good and bad characteristics and allows bad ones to come out so you can deal with them. Good for all psychic abilities and shamanic visions. Helps inhibition.

Boulder opal

A variety of **opal** found in cracks or as coatings in and around ironstone and sandstone boulders.

Common alternate name: Queensland opal
Common source: Australia
Astrological associations: Virgo, Libra, Scorpio
Chakra: throat

Healing qualities
Good for sexual attraction, faithfulness, hope, purity, and mental clarity.

Physical: good for eyesight. Protects from disease.
Emotional/spiritual: good for emotional security, spiritual development, inner beauty, prophecy, past-life recall, and the aura. Brings the sub-conscious into the conscious mind.

Fire opal

A variety of **opal** that exhibits fire.

Common sources: Australia, Mexico
Astrological associations: Cancer, Leo, Libra, Sagittarius, Pisces
Chakra: brow

Healing qualities

Good for intuition, insight and bringing variety to life.
Physical: good for energy, eyesight, and the central nervous system. Helps emphysema.
Emotional/spiritual: good for burn-out, 21st-century stress, meditation, spiritual vitality, and all psychic abilities.

Leopard skin rhyolite

A variety of **rhyolite**.

Common alternate name: leopard skin jasper
Common source: Mexico
Astrological association: Sagittarius
Chakra: base

Healing qualities

Physical: speeds the replication of genetic material, so excellent for the development of babies. Good for post-operative healing.
Emotional/spiritual: good for self-healing, shamanism, and connecting to/communicating with totem animals.

Warning: this stone speeds the growth of any virus or bacteria so do not use in cases of HIV/AIDS, cancer, or viral or bacterial infection.

Chalcopyrite

Occurs as octahedral crystals, masses and tetrahedral crystals with sphenoid faces. Colors include gold, blue, green, and purple – usually bright iridescent. Color is produced by natural oxidation of the surface. Scratching may remove bright colors to leave gray rock.

Common sources: Brazil, Mexico
Astrological association: Capricorn
Chakra: crown

Healing qualities

Good for perception. Good for martial arts and healing because it improves the flow of chi.
Physical: good for lungs and genetic material. Helps bronchitis, fever, inflammation, brain tumors, and the side effects of chemotherapy. Promotes hair growth. Aids detoxing.
Emotional/spiritual: balances color in energy and removes energy blocks. Helps all psychic abilities. Good for meditation and connection to the universe (helps you to reach and maintain a peak experience).

Rainbow fluorite

A variety of **fluorite**. Cubic or octahedral masses.

Common source: China
Astrological associations: Capricorn, Pisces
Chakras: heart, throat, brow, crown

Healing qualities

Good for focusing the mind, especially to deal with complex issues.
Physical: good for the eyes, ears, nose, and throat. Helps protect against disease and maintain health.

Titanium quartz

Quartz crystal bonded with titanium and niobium.

Common alternate names: flame aura quartz, rainbow quartz, rainbow aura quartz, aura quartz, royal aura
Common sources: Arkansas (USA) or Minas Gerais (Brazil)
Astrological associations: all star signs
Chakras: all

Healing qualities
A "feel better" crystal. Good for change, making career decisions and seeing another's point of view.
Physical: prevents illness. Good for body fluids. Helps fever, dehydration, water retention, bone cancer, acquired immuno-deficiency syndrome (AIDS), and multiple sclerosis (MS).
Emotional/spiritual: centers emotions when you feel all over the place. Good for meditation. Stimulates energy flow and helps you find your own true path through life. Helps you to see auras.

Sardonyx

A variety of **onyx** that contains **carnelian** and has black, red, brown, white, and clear bands.

Common source: India
Astrological association: Aries
Chakra: sacral

Healing qualities
Good for socializing, marriage, and other co-habiting relationships. Brings courage, luck, and protects you against crime.
Emotional/spiritual: helps hesitation.

Watermelon tourmaline

Green or blue **tourmaline** with pink or red center running through part or all of the crystal.

Common sources: Brazil, Pakistan
Astrological associations: Gemini, Virgo
Chakra: heart

Healing qualities
A "feel better" stone that is good for love, fun, humor, and seeing the funny side of any situation. Helps discretion and indiscretion. Reversed watermelon tourmaline is good for facilitating communication and travel.
Physical: good for the heart and lungs (**lime green tourmaline** – often with white center – is good for heart conditions). Reversed watermelon tourmaline is good for the reflexes and the absorption of food, and helps in accidents.
Emotional/spiritual: good for the emotions and the higher-self. Helps nervousness. Reversed watermelon tourmaline is good for stillness and synchronicity.
Lime green tourmaline is very gentle and calming, especially for the emotions.

Tiger iron

Tiger's eye, jasper and hematite banded in colors of yellow/brown, red, and black/gray.

Common source: Australia
Astrological association: Leo
Chakra: base

Healing qualities
Good for artistic ability, creativity and vitality. Encourages survival instincts.
Physical: good for the health of the muscles and blood. Helps vitamin B deficiency and anemia. Aids steroid production.

Multicolored

Agate

A variety of **chalcedony** found in masses and usually banded or patterned in many colors (see also specific **agates**).

Common source: worldwide
Astrological association: Gemini
Chakras: see specific **agates**

Healing qualities

Good for balancing sexual energy, faithfulness in relationships, and promoting natural talents.
Physical: good for sight and the health of the lymphatic system, colon, pancreas, and circulation. Helps gastroenteritis, irritable bowel syndrome (IBS), wind pains, and varicose veins.
Emotional/spiritual: good for chaneling, and emotional security and energy. Strengthens the aura and acts as a shield. Facilitates self-diagnosis during meditation.

Chalcedony

A form of **quartz** found in masses, with mineral inclusions that produce various colors such as white, pink, blue, and red (although, theoretically, chalcedony can be any color). Other varieties include **agate, bloodstone, carnelian, chrysoprase, flint, jasper, onyx, sardonyx,** and **petrified wood.**

Common source: worldwide
Astrological associations: Cancer, Sagittarius
Chakra: varies with variety and color

Healing qualities

Good for using in ceremonies. Promotes nurture and mental stability.
Physical: good for bone marrow. Helps drug addiction and addictive behavior, obsessive compulsive disorder (OCD), senility, dementia, obesity, and weight loss.
Emotional/spiritual: good for yin/yang balance, stress, and irritability. Facilitates telepathy.

Onyx

A multicolored, layered variety of **chalcedony**. May be black, gray, white, blue, brown, yellow, red, and orange.

Common source: India
Astrological association: Leo
Chakra: base

Healing qualities

Good for decision-making. Brings luck and happiness in the home.
Physical: good for bone marrow and feet.
Emotional/spiritual: helps grief and lack of self control. Helps you take charge of situations. Good for yin/yang balance, contact with "god", and connecting you to your roots.

Jasper

A variety of opaque **chalcedony** that may be **red, yellow, green**, brown, blue, and purple, sometimes with mixed colors and patterns, including **mookaite, orbicular jasper,** brecciated jasper, starry jasper with pyrite inclusions, and **picture jasper.**

Common sources: worldwide
Astrological association: Leo
Chakra: base (see also specific **jaspers**)

Healing qualities

Good for dowsing and diagnosis. Helps you to achieve goals.
Physical: helps prevent illness and acts as a general tonic when you are feeling down with minor illness. Good for the nerves, bladder, spleen, stomach, kidneys, liver, bile ducts, mineral balance, and sense of smell. Helps bronchitis, backache, cramps, wind pains, colds, flu, jaundice, and multiple sclerosis (MS). Useful during fasting.
Emotional/spiritual: helps loneliness and keeps your spirits up. Good for yin/yang balance and the aura.

Tourmaline

Vertically striated prismatic crystals. Varieties include: green **verdelite**, blue **indicolite**, pink **elbaite**, red **rubellite**, yellow **tsilasite**, black **schorl**, brown **dravite**, green or blue with pink center **watermelon** or colors reversed, bi-colors, tri-colors, **lime green** often with white center, colorless **achroite**, and lavender (a new find).

Common sources: Brazil, Pakistan,
Astrological association: Libra
Chakra: all (see specific varieties)

Healing qualities

Good for inspiration, connection, awareness, creativity, new challenges, and negotiation skills. Good for laughter therapy and use in groups. Enhances healing ability and offers protection on all levels from simple accidents to psychic attack. Tourmaline wand crystals (long, thin crystals) focus energy to areas where it is most needed and are good for affirmations and aura healing. Bi-color and tri-color tourmaline have the healing qualities of all the colors exhibited.

Physical: good for mental health and healing. Good for the digestion and the health of the bladder and lymphatic system. Helps schizophrenia and low blood pressure. Aids detoxing.

Emotional/spiritual: calming and good for self-confidence, balance, and removing blockages. Helps fear, obstructiveness, victim mentality, negativity, breakdown, and worrying too much what others think. Relieves a restless or troubled mind. Good for the inner self, yin/yang balance, the aura, all psychic abilities, and left/right brain activity.

Fluorite

Cubic, octahedral and rhombododecahedral crystals and masses. Colors include **purple**, **clear**, **blue**, **green**, **yellow**, brown, pink, red, black, and **rainbow fluorite**, which may include green, purple, blue and clear/colorless bands in the same specimen.

Common alternate name: fluor spar
Common sources: China, Europe, Mexico, South Africa, UK, USA
Astrological associations: Capricorn, Pisces
Chakra: brow

Healing qualities

Focuses the mind and creates order out of chaos. Good for decisions, concentration and relationships. Useful in groups.

Physical: good for the blood vessels, bones, spleen and teeth. Helps colds, flu, virulent infections, early stages of cancer, herpes, ulcers, weight gain, backache, lumbago, and eating disorders, such as anorexia and bulimia. Aids detox. Useful for carers working with infectious diseases. Alleviates the tiring effect of working at a computer screen.
Emotional/spiritual: good for meditation. Helps overexcitement and stress (allows the mind to work effectively in stressful situations).

Rhyolite

Mixture of feldspar and **quartz** in many color patterns including white, gray, red **leopard skin**, and green **rainforest**.

Common source: Mexico
Astrological association: Sagittarius
Chakra: base

Healing qualities

Good for change, creativity and finding answers to problems.
Physical: good for veins, stamina and muscle tone. Offers insight into causes of dis-ease. Helps chills, skin rashes, and vitamin B deficiency.
Emotional/spiritual: good for yin/yang balance. Helps you access past issues and find time to meditate.

Calcite

Masses, stalactites, scalenohedral, and rhombohedral crystals. Common colors include **green**, **blue**, yellow, **golden**, **orange**, clear **Iceland spa**, **white**, brown, pink, **red**, **black**, and gray.

Common source: worldwide
Astrological association: Cancer
Chakras: all (see specific varieties)

Healing qualities

A "feel better" stone that is useful for teaching and studying, especially art and science. Good for seeing the bigger picture.
Physical: good for the kidneys, pancreas and spleen. Helps bone growths and calcium deficiency.
Emotional/spiritual: calming and good for the emotions and yin/yang balance. Helps stress, over-enthusiasm and fear. Good for astral travel and channeling.

Zincite

Hexagonal crystals, masses, and layered "plates". May be colorless, red, orange, yellow, or green.

Common source: Poland
Astrological associations: Taurus, Libra
Chakras: base, sacral

Healing qualities

Good for relationships, vitality, personal power, creativity, removing energy blocks, mental clarity, and perception. Creates a healing environment and is useful in groups.
Physical: good for the hair, skin, prostate gland, and nerve impulses.
Emotional/spiritual: useful for catharsis.

Gypsum

Masses, fibers, and prismatic, needle-like, and tabular crystals. May be white, colorless/clear, green, brown/yellow, gray, pink, blue, red, brown, black, or orange. **Selenite** is the crystalline form of gypsum. Alabaster is the massive form. Gypsum is the fibrous form.

Common source: worldwide
Astrological association: Aries
Chakra: crown

Healing qualities

Brings luck. Good for moving forward in life. Useful in ceremonies.
Physical: good for fertility and skin elasticity. Helps psoriasis. Strengthens bones.
Emotional/spiritual: good for magic and connection.

Blue

Blue lace agate

A pale blue and white banded variety of **agate**.

Common source: South Africa
Astrological association: Pisces
Chakra: throat

Healing qualities

Improves communication on all levels.
Physical: good for the eyesight, speech, nails, and pancreas. Helps arthritis, stammer, fluid retention, trapped nerves, skin growths, and broken bones and fractures. Soothes tired eyes (as an elixir).
Emotional/spiritual: gentle and calming. Brings balance and emotional stability.
Raises your spiritual level and improves communication of spiritual ideas. Assists with attunement.

Angelite

Blue/white nodules, masses and, occasionally, crystals.

Common source: Peru
Astrological association: Aquarius
Chakra: throat

Healing qualities

Good for awareness, protection (as an elixir) and feelings of security. Useful for people who work with numbers. Improves communication on all levels.
Physical: good for the senses, throat, thymus, blood vessels, and hemoglobin. Acts as an insect repellent (as a topical elixir). Helps infectious diseases.
Emotional/spiritual: comforts grief and helps anger.

Improves communication with spirits. Helps to connect you to your angels, guardians, and totem animals. Assists channeling. Good for telepathy, balance, astral travel, re-birthing, and psychic and spiritual healing.

Aquamarine

A blue/green variety of **beryl**.

Common sources:
Afghanistan, Brazil,
Namibia, Pakistan,
USA
Astrological associations:
Aries, Gemini, Pisces
Chakra: throat

Healing qualities

Protects travelers. Good for the brain and intellect. Helps study, communication, and courage. Builds tolerance and responsibility. Makes things happen.
Physical: good for the kidneys, lymph, body fluids, blood, teeth, and eyes. Helps swollen glands, water retention, and swelling. Improves eyesight. Cooling in hot climates.
Emotional/spiritual: brings calm, compassion, spiritual awareness, and development, and reveals truth about yourself. Helps judgmental attitude. Brings you in contact with your inner and higher self. Good for centering and meditation. Gently washes away blocks in chakras. Clears pollutants (when used in visualization).

Azurite

Masses, nodules and, rarely, tabular, and prismatic crystals of azure or paler blues.

Common alternate name: blue malachite
Common sources: China, Morocco, USA
Astrological association: Sagittarius
Chakra: throat

Healing qualities

Enhances creativity. Known as the "Stone of Heaven".
Physical: good for blood strength and the nervous system. Helps arthritis.
Emotional/spiritual: good for psychic abilities. Helps you to express feelings, thoughts, and psychic information. Brings compassion and empathy.

Azurite/malachite

A combination of these two minerals in the form of masses or crystals.

Common sources: China, Morocco, USA
Astrological associations: Sagittarius, Capricorn
Chakras: brow, heart

Healing qualities

See also **azurite** and **malachite.** Brings individuality, freedom, rationality, and flexibility of mind and thought. Helps ego, conceit, arrogance, and vanity.
Physical: good for joints/flexibility, skin, bones, teeth, heart, circulation, gallbladder, and liver. Helps prevent and treat stress-related conditions, such as ulcers and asthma.
Emotional/spiritually: good for meditation; can bring the realization that sometimes the most profound changes are the simplest. Helps anxiety.

Blue calcite

Found in the form of blue masses.

Common source: Mexico
Astrological association: Cancer
Chakra: throat

Healing qualities

Good for the voice and communication.
Physical: good for the pharynx. Helps ADHA and throat infections, such as laryngitis.
Emotional/spiritual: spiritually calming.

Cavansite

Orthorhombic blue and white crystals, sometimes in flower formations.

Common source: India
Astrological association: Aquarius
Chakra: brow

Healing qualities

A "feel good" stone that is good for new ideas.
Physical: good for eyes, teeth, and blood. Helps osteoporosis.
Emotional/spiritual: good for all psychic abilities. Prevents healers picking up empathic pains from clients and taking home their issues.

Blue chalcedony

A light blue variety of **chalcedony.**

Common source: South Africa
Astrological associations: Cancer, Sagittarius
Chakra: throat

Healing qualities

Good for communication.
Physical: helps alcoholism.
Emotional/spiritual: good for dealing with childhood issues. Facilitates emotional expression.

Celestite

Tabular orthorhombic crystals, nodules, and masses in shades of blue. Crystals also occur in white, yellow, orange, red, and red-brown.

Common alternate name: celestine
Common source: Madagascar
Astrological association: Gemini
Chakra: brow

Healing qualities

Good for creative expression, speech, and clear thought, especially about complex ideas. Promotes respectful love and natural abilities. Good for music and art.
Physical: good for hearing. Helps with physical pain, mental disorders, and eye problems. Aids detoxing.
Emotional/spiritual: good for relaxation, dreams and dream recall, meditation, astral travel, and yin/yang balance. Helps with stress, worries, despair, and nightmares. Linked very strongly to angels.

Chalcanthite

Stunning blue flattened crystals, masses, stalactites, and fibers. The natural crystal is very rare but it can be easily grown in a laboratory – even in a garage. Chalcanthite is water soluble, so take care when cleansing (store away from humidity and sunlight).

Common source: USA (but can be made anywhere)
Astrological association: Aquarius
Chakra: throat

Healing qualities

Good for elocution and communication on all levels. Helps you achieve goals and make choices.
Physical: helps arthritis, water retention, and reproductive disorders. Lowers free radicals and cholesterol. **No elixir**

Covellite

Plates, masses, and, occasionally, crystals. Indigo blue, sometimes with iridescence of other rainbow colors.

Common alternate name: covelline
Common source: USA
Astrological association: Sagittarius
Chakra: brow

Healing qualities

Good for inward reflection, mental clearing, and helping you to speak your mind. Helps vanity and problem-solving. Enables miracles to happen and dreams to come true.
Physical: good for the eyes, ears, nose, mouth, and throat. Helps the birth process and cancer. Aids detox.
Emotional/spiritual: good for psychic abilities, meditation and re-birthing. **No elixir**

Dumortierite

Occurs in the form of blue and pink/brown masses.

Common source: Madagascar
Astrological association: Leo
Chakra: brow

Healing qualities

Helps you to speak your mind. Brings stamina and patience.
Physical: good for the ligaments and tendons. Helps you to understand the cause of disease.

Emotional/spiritual: brings quiet
confidence. Helps excitability and stubbornness.

Blue fluorite

A variety of **fluorite**. Cubic or octahedral masses

Common source: China
Astrological associations: Capricorn, Pisces
Chakra: throat

Healing qualities
Good for speech.
> *Physical:* good for the nose,
> tear ducts, inner ear, and
> throat.
> > *Emotional/spiritual:*
> > calming. Good for spirit
> > communication.

Hemimorphite

Botryoidal formations, tabular crystals and various
masses, including "fans". May be colorless, blue, green,
gray, or white.

Common source: China
Astrological association:
Libra
Chakra: throat

Healing qualities
A "feel better" stone that brings luck and creativity.
Physical: good for the blood. Helps ulcers, pain,
poisoning, vomiting, and venereal disease. Assists
dieting and weight loss. Maintains health.
Emotional/spiritual: brings self-confidence. Helps
selfishness, ego, and anger.

Iolite

Masses and short prismatic crystals exhibiting a
pleochroic effect. Colors include blue, brown, yellow,
violet, gray, and green.

Common alternate names: water sapphire,
cordierite, dichroite
Common source: India
*Astrological
associations:* Libra,
Sagittarius, Taurus
Chakra: brow

Healing qualities
Good for relationships and
money management. Facilitates painless change. Helps
irresponsibility.
Physical: good for the liver. Prevents illness. Helps
malaria and fever. Aids weight loss and detox. Some
people say it enables you to drink alcohol without
showing any effects.
Emotional/spiritual: good for emotional attachments,
yin/yang balance, the aura, astral travel, shamanic
visions and journeys, and living in the moment.
Helps visualization in guided meditations.

Blue opal

Blue masses, sometimes showing iridescence.

Common alternate name: Andean **opal**
Common source: Peru, Canada
Astrological associations: Taurus, Cancer
Chakra: throat

Healing qualities
Good for invisibility –
known as the "stone of
thieves". Good for
creativity, communication,
and the courage to speak
your mind. Facilitates problem solving and connection
with other people.
Physical: good for metabolism and iron balance. Helps
iron deficiency/excess, fatigue, tiredness, and hair loss.

Lapis lazuli

Rock, cubic and dodecahedral crystals, and masses. Almost always includes lazurite, **calcite**, and **pyrite**.

Common sources: Afghanistan, Chile
Astrological association: Sagittarius
Chakra: brow

Healing qualities

A "feel better" stone that brings vitality, wisdom, mental endurance, and creative expression. Promotes natural gifts and skills. Helps disorganization.
Physical: good for the immune system, throat, thymus, thyroid, Eustachian tube, bones, and bone marrow. Helps insomnia, vertigo, dizziness, hearing loss, and skeletal pain, such as backache. Aids detox. The crystals help to prevent illness and repair muscles, broken bones and fractures.
Emotional/spiritual: good for relaxation, relationships, dreams, yin/yang balance, and all psychic abilities. Helps depression.

Larimar

A variety of pectolite occurring in masses. Often found in radial groupings. Colors include blue, green, gray, and red (all possibly with white).

Common alternate name: pectolite
Common source: Dominican Republic
Astrological association: Leo
Chakra: heart

Healing qualities

Physical: good for the cartilage, hair, and feet.
Emotional/spiritual: soft gentle healing energy that soothes you and helps you see who you really are. Frees you from addiction to the material world. Good for earth healing. Helps guilt and aggression.

Pietersite

A variety of **tiger's eye**. Golden/brown or gray/blue, often in same specimen.

Common sources: South Africa, Namibia
Astrological association: Leo
Chakra: brow

Healing qualities

Good for creativity and sex. Allows you to see beauty in everything.
Physical: good for the pineal gland, pituitary gland (and other endocrine glands), metabolism, digestion, blood pressure, and temperature balance. Aids growth. Helps fever and hypothermia. Relieves the tiring effects of working at a computer screen.
Emotional/spiritual: aids creative visualization and visualization during guided meditation. Has a grounding effect. Helps fear. Gives access to akashic records.

Kyanite

Blade-type crystals, fibers and masses. Colors include blue, black, gray, white, green, yellow, and pink.

Common source: Brazil
Astrological associations: Aries, Taurus, Libra
Chakra: throat

Healing qualities

Good for perseverance, reason, mental stamina, the singing voice, and communication. Helps you to "talk your talk". Useful in sacred ceremonies.
Physical: good for the throat, muscles, neurological system, glands, and brain.
Emotional/spiritual: brings calm and tranquillity. Aligns chakras. Good for yin/yang balance, dream recall and understanding, psychic awareness, freeing energy blocks, connecting with spirit guides, and starting meditation. Assists with attunement.

Blue quartz

Clear or white **quartz** with **blue tourmaline (indicolite)** inclusions. Note: there are several other minerals called blue quartz that are not included here.

Common source: the only current source is Minas Gerais, Brazil
Astrological associations: Taurus, Libra
Chakra: throat

Healing qualities

Brings self-reliance, spontaneity, happiness, awareness, vitality, and wellbeing.
Physical: good for the spleen, endocrine system, blood, and metabolism.
Emotional/spiritual: good for emotional balance, awareness and energy shift. Brings bliss and connection to people, the universe, spirit, and god. Aids communication on all planes allowing you to express what's in your mind. Brings issues to the surface allowing it to clear, while keeping you grounded. Helps anger, introversion, apprehension, and anxiety. Assists telepathy and tarot card readings. Gives increased insight into divination.

Aqua aura

A **quartz** crystal bonded with **gold** giving beautiful, mostly clear blue crystals and clusters.

Common source: USA (from Arkansas or Brazilian quartz)
Astrological association: Leo
Chakras: brow, throat

Healing qualities

A "feel better" stone that is good for communication and protection.
Emotional/spiritual: good for the aura and all psychic abilities. Helps negativity, depression, sadness, loss, and grief.

Sapphire

A gem variety of corundum found in any color except red (**ruby**) blue, yellow oriental topaz, green oriental emerald, black, purple (violet) oriental amethyst, pink, and white.

Common sources: Sri Lanka, Madagascar, Thailand, India
Astrological associations: Virgo, Libra, Sagittarius
Chakra: brow

Healing qualities

Good for the fulfilment of ambitions, dreams and goals. Brings intuition, joy, fun, and wisdom.

Physical: good for the stomach, heart, hormones, and glands. Helps aging, backache, bleeding, infection, nausea, boils, and glandular fever. Has astringent properties.
Emotional/spiritual: good for emotional balance, control of desire, spiritual connection, seeing the beauty in everything, and accessing spirit guides. Helps depression, narrow-mindedness, and unhappiness. Sapphire is a "record-keeper" crystal which makes it valuable for connecting to spiritual wisdom including the akashic records and astral travel.
Star sapphires (they show asterism – star patterns) enhance all of the above qualities.

Shattuckite

A blue variety of plancheite found as masses or fibers.

Common source: USA
Astrological associations: Sagittarius, Aquarius
Chakras: throat, brow

Healing qualities

Good for communication.
Physical: a general tonic for minor illness (as an elixir). Helps hemophilia and tonsillitis. Aids blood clotting.
Emotional/spiritual: good for mediumship, channeling, automatic writing, tarot, runes, and any divination, including reading the entrails of sheep. Helps you to create your own reality.

Sodalite

Blue or blue and white masses, nodules and, rarely, dodecahedral and hexagonal prismatic crystals. May also be colorless, gray, green, yellow, white, or red.

Common source: Brazil
Astrological association: Sagittarius
Chakra: brow

Healing qualities

Good for ideas, perception, creative expression, and endurance. Useful in groups.
Physical: good for physical balance and the health of the metabolism and lymphatic system. Helps high blood pressure, insomnia, autism, aging, diabetes, and calcium deficiency. Assists the development of babies.
Emotional/spiritual: good for calming, self-esteem, mental health and healing, and communicating feelings. Helps confusion, inadequacy, mental unrest, oversensitivity, and fear.

Tanzanite

A variety of **zoisite** in the form of masses and prismatic striated crystals. May be blue, yellow, gray/blue, or purple.

Common source: Tanzania
Astrological associations: Gemini, Libra, Sagittarius
Chakras: throat, brow, crown

Healing qualities

Good for communication.
Physical: good for the skin and eyes. Helps exhaustion.
Emotional/spiritual: good for meditation, visualization, magic, and all psychic abilities. Helps access to spirit guides.

Hawk's eye

A blue variety of **tiger's eye.**

Common source: South Africa
Astrological association: Capricorn
Chakras: brow, throat

Healing qualities

Physical: good for the throat, pharynx, and peristalsis. Helps laryngitis.
Emotional/spiritual: good for all psychic abilities. Helps disarray.

Blue topaz

Blue prismatic crystals and alluvial pebbles

Common sources: Afghanistan, Brazil
Astrological associations: Sagittarius, Virgo
Chakra: throat

Healing qualities
Good for clear communication.
Physical: good for balancing the body.
Emotional/spiritual: good for balancing the mind and spirit. Helps arrogance and obsessive passion.

Indicolite

A variety of blue **tourmaline**.

Common sources: Brazil, Pakistan
Astrological associations: Taurus, Libra
Chakra: throat, brow

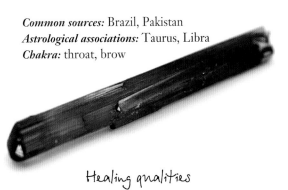

Healing qualities
Good for environmental issues and saving the planet. Helps communication, intuition, thought, ideas, and creativity. Enables you to "talk your talk and walk your walk".
Physical: good for the lungs, throat, larynx, esophagus, thymus, thyroid, eyes, and brain.
Emotional/spiritual: helps all psychic abilities.

Turquoise

Blue, green or blue/green masses, crusts and, rarely, small short prismatic crystals.

Common sources: China, Myanmar, Tibet, USA
Astrological associations: Scorpio, Sagittarius, Pisces
Chakra: throat

Healing qualities
Protects travelers (whether your journey is local or across the world) and property, and keeps you safe from accidents. Good for creative expression, courage, communication, wisdom, compassion, romance, love, and friendship. Helps public speaking and writing. Gets rid of pollution. Allows you to see the beauty in everything.
Physical: a multi-purpose healer for the body. Good for the muscles, circulation, lungs, throat, and the absorption of nutrients. Helps general malaise, arthritis, rheumatism, skeletal pain, such as backache, flu, allergies, asthma, bronchitis, breathing, tissue regeneration, weight gain, wind pains, headaches, whiplash, air sickness, cataracts, wounds, post-operative recovery, and stress-related skin disorders (as an elixir). Aids detox. Alleviates the harmful effects of radiation.
Emotional/spiritual: good for emotional balance, meditation (grounding peak experiences), spirit contact, all psychic abilities, astral travel, spirituality, peace of mind, and yin/yang balance. Offers the mental and spiritual clarity to see your own path in life. Helps suspicious minds and negativity.

Ametrine

A mixture of **amethyst** and **citrine** – purple and gold in color.

Common source: Bolivia
Astrological association: Libra
Chakras: solar plexus, crown

Healing qualities

Brings peace and tranquillity. Good for inspiration, creativity, and change. Removes physical, mental, emotional, and spiritual blockages. Overcomes prejudice, ignorance, and obstructiveness.
Physical: repairs damage to DNA. Helps organ transplants.
Emotional/spiritual: promotes an intellectual understanding of spirituality. Speeds the meditation process (you get to your own deepest or highest state in less time). Good for astral travel, yin/yang balance, and the aura. Relieves tension.

Charoite

Found in the form of violet masses, sometimes with white **quartz** and black manganese inclusions.

Common source: Russia
Astrological associations: Scorpio, Sagittarius
Chakra: crown

Healing qualities

Good for intuition, analysis, seeing opportunities, moving forward, and increasing your attention span.
Physical: good for slowing the pulse rate, and the health of the eyes and heart. Helps general aches and pains, headaches, liver damage (sclerosis of the liver), pancreatic damage, autism, and attention deficit hyperactivity disorder (ADHD). Aids detox.
Emotional/spiritual: good for meditation and clairvoyance. Facilitates living in the moment. Helps to break unwanted cycles, release you from old relationships, and bring your spiritual experiences into your physical world.

Purple fluorite

A purple variety of **fluorite**.

Common sources: China, Mexico, UK, USA
Astrological associations: Capricorn, Pisces
Chakra: crown

Healing qualities

Good for communication and new lessons (spiritual or physical).
Physical: good for bones and bone marrow. Helps most dis-ease on a deeper spiritual level.

Lepidolite

Found as masses and layered plates (or "books"), and short prismatic and tabular crystals. May be colorless, lavender (pink to purple), yellow, gray, or white.

Common source: Brazil
Astrological association: Libra
Chakras: heart, brow

Healing qualities

Good for learning, studying, change, and awareness. Helps to produce an abundant crop yield.
Physical: good for digestion and the nerves. Useful during childbirth. Helps tendonitis, cramps, constipation, erratic heartbeat, addictions, and wrinkles.
Emotional/spiritual: calming. Good for astral travel and re-birth. Helps distrust, depression, stress (and related conditions), addictive personalities, and transitions such as death/dying.

Spirit quartz

A variety of **amethyst** (purple) or **quartz** (white), sometimes with orange/brown iron inclusions or surface staining.

Common source: South Africa
Astrological associations: Virgo, Capricorn, Aquarius, Pisces
Chakra: crown

Healing qualities

Brings patience, abundance and a sense of belonging. Useful in groups and work environments. Good for sports and team-building. Offers protection.
Physical: good for fertility. Helps skin allergies and aids detox.

Emotional/spiritual: releases and revitalizes emotions. Good for extra-sensory perception (ESP), flow, self-esteem, meditation, astral travel, re-birthing, and dreams. Facilitates access to your inner/higher-self, dark side, past experiences, and past lives. Helps loneliness, grief, obsessiveness, and fear of success.

Sugilite

Found as violet masses and, rarely, tiny crystals.

Common alternate names: lavulite, royal lavulite, royal azel
Common source: South Africa
Astrological association: Virgo
Chakra: crown

Healing qualities

Good for mental balance, confidence, creativity, and courage. Allows eccentricities to express themselves.
Physical: good for whole body healing and the mind-body link in dis-ease. Good for the adrenal, pineal, and pituitary glands. Helpful in the treatment of most illnesses, particularly epilepsy. Can relieve headaches (hold the stone to the pain) and physical discomfort (hold the stone in the hand). Helps children with learning difficulties, including dyslexia.

Emotional/spiritual: good for spiritual love, spirit contact and finding your life path. Helps with hostility, anger, jealousy, forgiveness, prejudice, and despair.

Anhydrite

Clear/gray/white tabular crystals and masses.

Common source: Mexico
Astrological associations:
Cancer, Scorpio,
Pisces
Chakras: sacral,
solar plexus

Healing qualities

Physical: good for physical strength and stamina. Good for the throat. Helps water retention and swelling.
Emotional/spiritual: good for acceptance and the release of past issues. Helps you to cope with and understand the dying process.

Apophyllite

Cubic and pyramidal crystals, druses, and masses. Commonly white or colorless and, rarely, green. See also **zeolite**.

Common source: India
Astrological associations: Gemini, Libra
Chakras: brow, crown

Healing qualities

Good for travel, truth, and brain power. Pyramidal crystals help preserve food.
Physical: good for sight. Pyramidal crystals can aid rejuvenation of the body.
Emotional/spiritual: good for reflection, astral travel, scrying (a type of divination), and clairvoyance. Helps you connect to spirit and maintain a meditative state after meditation.

Azeztulite

A colorless/white variety of **quartz** with traces of beryllium.

Common source: USA
Astrological associations: all
Chakras: all

Healing qualities

Helps you make the best of all situations, including bad ones. Channels any type of energy, so will help with all healing.
Physical: helps cancer.
Emotional/spiritual: restores "the will" in terminally ill patients. Aids visualization and premonition (place the stone on the brow chakra). Good for meditation – starts and speeds access to peak experiences.

Barite

Tabular crystals, layered plates, and fibrous masses. Also found in the form of a rose or rosette pattern. May be colorless, blue, white, gray, yellow, or brown.

Common alternate names: barytes, baryte, barytine
Common sources: worldwide
Astrological association: Aquarius
Chakra: throat

Healing qualities

Good for friendship, harmony, love, and insight into relationships. Promotes communication of ideas and thoughts. Motivates you to take action.
Physical: good for the throat and eyesight. Aids detox. Helps recovery from addiction.
Emotional/spiritual: good for catharsis, spiritual connection, and finding your spiritual path in life. Helps shyness.

Iceland spa

Clear rhombohedral crystals that show double refraction (you see two images through the crystal).

Common source: Mexico
Astrological associations: Gemini, Cancer
Chakras: all

Healing qualities

Good for decision making and clear thinking.
Physical: aids detox.
Emotional/spiritual: calms the mind. Helps you cope with mind games and lets you see two sides of an argument.

White calcite

Found as white "dogtooth" crystals.

Common source: Brazil
Astrological association: Cancer
Chakra: crown

Healing qualities

Physical: good for the kidneys, liver, and lymphatic system. Aids detox.
Emotional/spiritual: clears the mind and helps you find answers. Good for meditation.

Cerussite

Lead ore (sometimes containing silver) crystallizing as orthorhombic crystals in several forms: single crystals, clusters, snowflakes or stars, and those like trees with icicles. May be clear, white, gray, black, or yellow.

Common source: Namibia
Astrological association: Virgo
Chakra: base

Healing qualities

Good for change, decision-making, and taking responsibility.
Brings wisdom, creativity, tact, and the ability to listen. Useful during ceremonies and rituals. Helps writing, homesickness, and relationships. Can get rid of pests.
Physical: helps insomnia, Alzheimer's disease and Parkinson's disease. Restores vitality after illness.
Emotional/spiritual: good for grounding. Helps combat tension, anxiety, and introversion. Facilitates access to past lives.
No elixir. Wash hands after contact with lead ore.

Cleavelandite

A platy variety of albite, usually white in color.

Common alternate name: clevelandite (this is a common misspelling)
Common sources: Brazil, USA
Astrological association: Libra
Chakra: crown

Healing qualities

Offers protection for travelers. Helps you to accept others and achieve goals. Good for relationships.
Physical: good for blood vessels in the brain. Helps arteriosclerosis, strokes, heart disease, degenerative joint disease, allergies, skin conditions, ulcerative colitis, and disorders of cell membranes. Tackles underlying causes of stress-related conditions, such as asthma.

Coral

The remains of marine colonial animals. Colors include white, black, pink, red, and blue.

Common source: many, but not all, coral species are now protected by law, which means there is little new legal stock available. Check that the coral you buy is legal stock. For example, many stockists have old supplies of "fish tank" coral that was legitimately imported prior to legal restrictions.
Astrological association: Pisces
Chakra: crown

Healing qualities

A good first stone for children – it protects them in the adventure playground of life. Brings wisdom, intuition, diplomacy, and imagination. Helps to dispel other people's issues. Useful for people in the caring professions or manual workers.
Physical: good for bones, teeth, digestion, circulation, spinal canal, thalamus, and the sense of smell. Helps weight gain, malnutrition, lethargy, insanity, abdominal colic, gum disease, whiplash and post-operative healing.
Emotional/spiritual: good for emotions, visualization, clairaudience, and energy flow. Helps depression, negativity, and concern about what others think. Repairs the aura after physical trauma.

Dalmatian stone

A mixture of **quartz**, microcline and **tourmaline**. White with black dots (named after the Dalmatian breed of dog).

Common source: Mexico
Astrological association: Gemini
Chakra: base

Healing qualities

Protects from physical danger. Connects physical and spiritual energy. Helps learning and achieving goals. Good for relationships and letting go of the past. Brings happiness, devotion, and composure.
Physical: good for cartilage and physical stamina. Soothes nerves, muscle sprains, and cramps.
Emotional/spiritual: calming. Good for yin/yang balance. Helps negativity.

Danburite

Clear/white, pink, yellow, and lilac prismatic striated crystals.

Common sources: Mexico, USA
Astrological association: Leo
Chakra: crown

Healing qualities

Good for socialization.
Physical: good for the gallbladder and liver. Helps muscle stiffness and weight gain. Aids detox.
Emotional/spiritual: helps post-operative depression, and getting back into the world after an absence (whether due to breakdown, drug problems, hospitalization or other reasons).

Diamond

Octahedral, dodecahedral and trapezohedral crystals. May be clear, white, yellow, blue, brown, pink, red, orange, and green.

Common sources: Australia, Brazil, India, Russia, S. Africa, Venezuela
Astrological associations: Aries, Taurus, Leo
Chakras: all

Healing qualities

Brings protection, purity, creativity, imagination, ingenuity, invention, abundance, change, and new beginnings. Good for right/left brain activity, love, relationships, and starting new projects. Brings positive physical and spiritual energy to any situation. Clears mental obstacles and allows you to like yourself. Increases the effects of all other crystals.
Physical: good for sight and metabolism. Aids detox. Helps recovery from poisoning.
Emotional/spiritual: good for spiritual awareness and the aura. Helps negativity, cowardice, anger, and childhood issues.

Herderite

Prismatic and tabular crystals, and fibrous masses. Green to pale yellow; also purple (recently discovered).

Common sources: Brazil, Germany, Pakistan, UK, USA
Astrological association: Aries
Chakra: brow

Healing qualities

Brings passion. Good for leadership. Useful in groups.
Physical: good for the pancreas, spleen and gallbladder.
Emotional/spiritual: good for behavior patterns. Promotes all psychic abilities.

Dolomite

Rhombohedral and prismatic white, gray, green, red, pink, brown, and black crystals and masses.

Common sources: Morocco
Astrological association: Aries
Chakra: crown

Healing qualities

Encourages original thought. Balances energy and removes

blockages. Good for inventors and writers.
Physical: good for the adrenal glands, urogenital system, bones, nails, teeth, skin, and muscles. Helps acidity, chills, and cancer.
Emotional/spiritual: helps grief and sadness.

Clear fluorite

Forms cubic, octahedral, and rhombododecahedral crystals and masses.

Common sources: China, UK
Astrological associations: Capricorn, Pisces
Chakra: crown

Healing qualities

Physical: good for the eyes.
Emotional/spiritual: good for the aura. Links physical with spiritual experiences.

Goshenite

A colorless variety of **beryl** in the form of prismatic crystals.

Common sources: Russia, China
Astrological association: Libra
Chakra: brow

Healing qualities

Good for relationships and creativity. Helps you to express yourself and live life in the way that you want to. Enables you to move forward.
Physical: good for the legs. Helps attention deficit hyperactivity disorder (ADHD) and autism.

Herkimer diamond

A clear, stubby double-terminated **quartz** crystal.

Common source: the sole source is Herkimer County, New York State, USA. Other "diamond-style" quartz crystals are available from Pakistan, Mexico, and Romania; although these may be wonderful crystals, they should not be confused with Herkimer diamonds.

Astrological association: Sagittarius
Chakra: crown

Healing qualities

Encourages spontaneity. Good for memory and new beginnings.
Physical: good for the metabolism and genetic material. Aids detox. Offers protection from radiation. Helps get rid of toxins.
Emotional/spiritual: good for relaxation, being in the moment and all psychic abilities. Helps stress, fear, and tension. Brings attunement to energies, people, places, deities – useful during ceremonies and reiki.

Howlite

Occurs in the form of nodules, masses and, rarely, crystals. Howlite is often dyed and used to imitate more expensive stones.

Common source: USA
Astrological association: Gemini
Chakra: crown

Healing qualities

Good for calm communication, discernment, memory, study, and action. Helps you to reach your goals. Combats selfishness, boisterousness, and vulgarity.

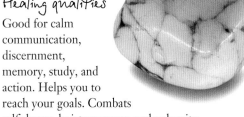

Physical: good for the teeth, bones, immune system, and circulation. Helps physical pain.
Emotional/spiritual: good for emotional expression. Helps stress and anger.

Magnesite

Occurs in the form of masses and nodules that look a bit like 200 million-year-old chewing gum! It also occurs in the form of rhombohedral, prismatic, tabular, and scalenohedral crystals, but this is rare. Usually white, but also gray, brown, or yellow.

Common sources: worldwide
Astrological association: Aries
Chakra: crown

Healing qualities

Good for love and passion.
Grounds the intellect.
Physical: good for the bones, teeth, tendons, ligaments, cardiac arteries, and cholesterol levels. Aids detox at a cellular level. Balances body temperature. Helps convulsions, premenstrual syndrome (PMS), body odor, arteriosclerosis, angina, fever, chills, and hypothermia.
Emotional/spiritual: good for visualization and meditation.

Moonstone

A variety of feldspar that exhibits the optical effect of chatoyancy. Colors include white, cream, yellow, brown, blue, green, or rainbow (white with a blue color flash).

Common source: India
Astrological associations: Cancer, Libra, Scorpio
Chakra: sacral

Healing qualities

Good for wisdom, passion, change, new beginnings, endings, intuition, insight, and creativity. Offers protection to travelers. Brings good luck and a happy home.

Physical: good for the circulation, skin, hair, eyes, pituitary gland, and fertility. Helps women in terms of pregnancy, childbirth, female qualities, hormones, and sexuality; regulates the menstrual cycle and eases menopausal symptoms, premenstrual syndrome (PMS), and period pains. Promotes a youthful appearance. Helps constipation, water retention, swelling, insect bites, and anaphylactic shock (an extreme allergic reaction).

Emotional/spiritual: soothing and good for the inner self and emotions generally. Releases energy blocks. Brings calm, control, balance, confidence, composure, peace of mind, and caring and compassion. Helps oversensitivity, pessimism, and combats cycles/repeated patterns.

Okenite

Occurs in white/clear fibrous masses that resemble snowballs or puffballs.

Common source: India
Astrological associations: Virgo, Sagittarius
Chakra: crown

Healing qualities

Brings purity, open-mindedness, and stamina (physical, emotional, mental, and spiritual).
Physical: good for youthfulness, blood flow, mammary glands, and circulation in the arms. Helps aging, fever, boils, and diarrhea.
Emotional/spiritual: gives you the equivalent of a big cuddle. Good for karma, channeling, and flow through life. Helps self-doubt, denial, hate, and compulsive behavior patterns.

Common opal

A variety of **opal** that, unlike other varieties, does not exhibit iridescence (fire).

Common alternate name: potch
Common sources: UK, USA
Astrological associations: Cancer, Libra
Chakra: sacral

Healing qualities

Brings vitality. Good for business relationships.
Emotional/spiritual: good for yin/yang balance. Combats self-importance.

Pearl

Round stones that are formed inside oyster shells. May be white, black, gray, pinkish, or yellowish.

Common sources: Japan, China
Astrological associations: Gemini, Cancer
Chakra: sacral

Healing qualities

Brings wisdom and focuses the mind. Good for chastity and purity.
Physical: good for digestion, fertility, childbirth, and feminine sexuality and qualities. Combats biliousness and bloating.
Emotional/spiritual: good for emotional control. Helps irritability and anti-social behavior.

Petalite

Occurs in clear, white, pink, gray, green/white, and red/white masses.

Common sources: Brazil, Madagascar
Astrological association: Leo
Chakra: crown

Healing qualities

Combats clumsiness. Gives you the courage of your convictions.
Physical: good for the eyelids and eyebrows, and muscle and joint flexibility. Aids detox. Helps acquired immuno-deficiency syndrome (AIDS), myalgic encephalomyelitis (ME), chronic fatigue syndrome (CFS), cancer, and tumors.
Emotional/spiritual: brings peace of mind, and spiritual connection to "god", angels, spirit guides, and totem animals. Good for meditation (helps you to stay grounded), the aura, yin/yang balance, shamanic vision quests, astral travel, and all psychic abilities.

Phenacite

Rhombohedral and slender prismatic crystals, masses, and fibrous spherical structures. May be colorless or tinted.

Common sources: Brazil, Madagascar, Russia, USA, Zimbabwe
Astrological association: Gemini
Chakras: crown, brow

Healing qualities

Focuses the mind. Good for awareness, and mental health and healing.
Physical: helps with all physical healing.
Emotional/spiritual: good for meditation and energy cleansing.

Metamorphosis quartz

A variety of **quartz** with several trace minerals. Occurs in the form of masses and, occasionally, prismatic crystals.

Common source: can only be sourced from two mines in Minas Gerais, Brazil.
Astrological association: Scorpio
Chakras: all

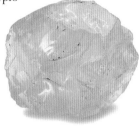

Healing qualities

Brings change and transformation – the ultimate crystal to work with if you want to change your life. Works well with **eudialyte,** which eases the discomfort that change can bring. Good for mental awareness.
Physical: good for stamina and the oxygenation of blood.
Emotional/spiritual: good for positive thinking and seeing auras. Combats negative, judgmental attitudes.

Tibetan quartz

Clear **quartz** crystals, often with black **hematite** inclusions.

Common source: can only be sourced from the Tibetan Himalayas (a lot of Chinese Himalayan quartz falsely claims to be from Tibet)
Astrological associations: all
Chakras: all

Healing qualities

A "feel good" stone. Helps you get to the point.
Emotional/spiritual: brings spiritual connection.

Angel aura quartz

A **quartz** crystal that is bonded with platinum and silver.

Common alternate name:
opal aura
Common source:
Arkansas, USA,
Brazil
*Astrological
associations:* all
Chakras: all

Healing qualities
Brings nurture,
harmony, love,
and peace. Good for people who work in the caring professions.
Physical: keeps you well.
Emotional/spiritual: brings access to angels, the angelic realms, and the akashic records. Good for empathy, karma, and aura protection.

Phantom quartz

A variety of **quartz** with colored "ghost-like" inclusions.

Common sources: Brazil, Madagascar, USA
Astrological associations: all
Chakras: heart, crown

Healing qualities
Helps you to see hidden
answers.
Emotional/spiritual:
good for
emotional clearing
and the inner-self.

Rutilated quartz

A variety of **quartz** with silver or golden threads of **rutile.**

Common alternate name: angel hair
Common source: Brazil
Astrological associations: all
Chakras: brow, crown

Healing qualities
Brings strength and
vitality. Good for mental
health and healing.
Physical: good for tissue
regeneration and the
immune system. Brings
a youthful appearance.
Activates the nerves.
Helps neuralgia,
Parkinson's disease,
weight gain, and aging.
Emotional/spiritual: brings balance and calm. Helps depression, mental breakdown, energy blockages, and negativity.

Snow quartz

A form of **quartz** that occurs in white masses.

Common alternate names: quartzite, milky quartz
Common source: USA, India
Astrological association: Capricorn
Chakra: crown

Healing qualities
Brings wisdom and
purity. Helps
study and
revision for
exams. Clears
the mind and
brings clarity
of thought.
Emotional/spiritual: helps negativity.

Tourmalinated quartz

A variety of **quartz** with black **tourmaline** rods growing through it.

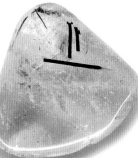

Common alternate name: tourmaline in quartz
Common source: Brazil
Astrological associations: all
Chakras: all

Healing qualities

Helps childhood experiences and behavior patterns. Good for problem-solving.
Physical: good for the nervous system. Helps nervous exhaustion.
Emotional/spiritual: helps depression and fear.

Scapolite

Occurs as masses and prismatic crystals that often exhibit the optical effect of chatoyancy (see **cat's eye**). May be colorless, white, yellow, pink, green, violet, gray, blue, red, or purple (recently discovered).

Common sources: Canada, Europe, Madagascar, USA
Astrological association: Taurus
Chakra: brow

Healing qualities

Good for change, problem-solving, and lateral thinking. Helps you to meet goals.
Physical: good for the bones, veins and eyes. Helps cataracts, glaucoma, dyslexia, and incontinence. Aids post-operative care.
Emotional/spiritual: supports you when feeling burdened. Good for dealing with past issues.

Selenite

A crystallized form of gypsum that is usually clear or white.

Common sources: Morocco, Mexico (for satin spa variety), Canada (for golden selenite variety)
Astrological association: Taurus (selenite is also linked with the moon – Selene is the goddess of the moon)
Chakra: crown

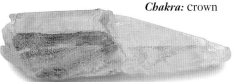

Healing qualities

Physical: good for sex drive, the menstrual cycle, longevity, skin elasticity, the spine, and a youthful appearance. Helps wrinkles, age spots and skin problems such as acne, eczema, psoriasis, and skin sensitivity. Helps loss of fertility, hair loss, epilepsy, and light sensitivity. Alleviates the effects of leakage from mercury amalgam fillings. Helps conditions that are associated with free radicals, including cancer and tumors.
Emotional/spiritual: helps abuse.

Stilbite

Occurs as white/clear plates, globes, radial structures, and thin tabular and rhombic cruciform crystals.

Common source: India
Astrological association: Aries
Chakras: throat, brow, crown

Healing qualities

Good for creativity, intuition, and grounding.
Physical: good for the tastebuds, brain, ligaments, and skin (enhances skin color/tan). Helps laryngitis and poisoning. Aids detox.

Topaz

Prismatic crystals and alluvial pebbles. May be clear, golden **imperial topaz**, **blue**, white, red/pink, brown, green, or purple (recently discovered).

Common alternate names: clear or silver topaz
Common sources: Brazil, Kenya, USA
Astrological association:
Sagittarius
Chakras: sacral, solar plexus

Healing qualities

This is a wish stone that is good for reasoning, creativity, creative expression, vitality, abundance, wealth, success, and individuality. Helps indecision and gives you the impetus you need to accomplish your goals.
Physical: brings general good health. Good for taste, the skin, lungs, and nerves. Aids detox. Combats the effects of pollution. Helps allergies, addiction, alcoholism, muscular back pain, gastroenteritis, tuberculosis (TB), myalgic encephalomyelitis (ME), wounds, tissue regeneration, and the common cold.
Emotional/spiritual: good for confidence, visualization, meditation, and absent/distant healing. Helps 21st century stress, negativity, and trepidation.

Achroite

A colorless variety of **tourmaline**.

Common source: Pakistan
Astrological association: Aquarius
Chakra: crown

Healing qualities
Brings inspiration, and clarity of mind and thought. Helps you to reach goals, and communicate on a profound level.
Emotional/spiritual: good for spiritual energy.

Ulexite

Silky clear or white fibrous masses.

Common alternate names: TV rock, TV stone, caveman's TV
Common source: USA
Astrological association: Gemini
Chakra: brow, crown

Healing qualities

Good for business pursuits, imagination, and creativity. Clears mental fog and brings clarity of mind.
Physical: good for the eyes. Aids detox. Tackles sources of dis-ease.
Emotional/spiritual: good for yin/yang balance, the inner-self, telepathy, visions, and clarity of spirit.

Zeolite

Formed from a group of minerals that commonly occur together. May be colorless, clear, white, blue, or peach. **Apophyllite**, **okenite**, **pectolite**, **prehnite**, and **stilbite** are all in the zeolite group.

Common source: India
Astrological associations: all
Chakra: depends on the specific mineral

Healing qualities
Improves your environment.
Physical: helps bloating, goiter, and alcoholism. Aids detox.
Emotional/spiritual: connects with reiki.

Black agate

A black variety of **agate**.

Common source: India
Astrological association: Capricorn
Chakra: base

Healing qualities
Good for
practicalities, the will
to live, and the
survival instinct.
Emotional/spiritual:
grounding. Brings inner strength.

Black banded agate

A variety of **agate** showing black and white banding.

Common source: India
Astrological association: Capricorn
Chakra: base

Healing qualities
Good for endurance, change, new beginnings, and
finding answers by seeing things differently.
Physical: good for death and the dying process.
Emotional/spiritual: good for
yin/yang balance.

Bixbyite

Black cubic crystals.

Common source: USA
Astrological association: Pisces
Chakras: brow, crown

Healing qualities

Good for creativity, intuition, imagination, adaptability,
teaching, writing, and art.
Physical: helps headaches and coping with pain.
Emotional/spiritual: grounding and centering. Good for
spirituality and starting meditation.

Black calcite

Black rhombohedral crystals.

Common source: Madagascar
Astrological association: Capricorn
Chakra: base

Healing qualities
Brings protection.
Good for female qualities
and sexual energy.
Physical: good for sexuality.
Emotional/spiritual: grounding. Good for inner
truth/knowing.

Cassiterite

Short prismatic crystals and masses. May be black, brown, or yellow.

Common alternate name: tinstone
Common source: UK
Astrological association: Sagittarius
Chakra: base

Healing qualities

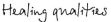

Good for vitality, optimism, intellect, and those who work with numbers. Brings protection from physical danger. Helps with rejection and prejudice.
Physical: good for the pancreas. Helps obesity, weight loss, and hormone imbalance,
Emotional/spiritual: grounding.

Goethite

Found as scales, fibers, prismatic crystals, needle-like structures, masses, radial stalactites, and "pipe organ" structures. May be black/brown, yellow, orange, or red.

Common sources: found in **amethyst** from Brazil and **quartz** from Madagascar
Astrological association: Aries
Chakra: brow

Healing qualities

Helps you to have fun and enjoy life.
Physical: good for the veins, ears, nose, throat, and digestive system. Helps anemia, abnormally heavy menstrual blood flow, and convulsions. Assists weight gain and body building.
Emotional/spiritual: good for psychic abilities, communication with angels and spirits, and clairaudience.

Jet

The fossilized remains of trees.

Common sources: UK, Canada
Astrological association: Capricorn
Chakra: base

Healing qualities

Good for sexual energy and wealth.
Physical: helps migraine, epilepsy, swollen glands, stomach ache, and the common cold.
Emotional/spiritual: brings energy that is grounded with calmness. Good for yin/yang balance, protection (against illness, violence and witchcraft – together with **red jasper**). Helps to alleviate depression and feelings of fear.

Larvakite

A black variety of **feldspar**, sometimes with sheen or iridescent flashes of color.

Common alternate name: Norwegian moonstone
Common source: Norway
Astrological associations: Leo, Scorpio, Sagittarius
Chakras: base, throat, brow, crown

Healing qualities

Physical: good for the lungs. Enhances sleep.
Emotional/spiritual: relaxing and grounding.
Enhances dreams, and understanding and insights from dreams. Brings emotions to the surface (like a volcano erupting) and then soothes the heart. Integrates the past with the present. Targets the base of the brain (the site of the ancient original brain and thought). Good for the aura, astral travel, and astral projection. Helps insecurity and apprehension.

Lodestone

Magnetic black/brown masses and octahedral crystals. The same mineral without the magnetism is called **magnetite**.

Common source: USA
Astrological associations: Gemini, Virgo
Chakra: base

Healing qualities

Good for finding direction. Brings receptivity and acceptance. Allows you to get the best from uncomfortable situations. Helps geopathic stress.
Physical: helps arthritis, rheumatism, and muscle aches and cramps.
Emotional/spiritual: grounding. Good for being in the moment, energy flow, and yin/yang balance. Helps insecurity, dependence, and confusion. Lifts burdens.

Magnetite

Black or brown octahedral crystals, masses, and dendrites. Specimens that exhibit magnetic polarity are known as **lodestone**.

Common source: USA
Astrological associations: Aries, Virgo, Capricorn, Aquarius
Chakra: base

Healing qualities

Good for protection, especially from empathic symptoms and other people's energy – useful among healers and those in the caring professions. Good for tenacity, endurance, desires, attracting love, and trusting your gut feelings.
Physical: good for the bones, hair, skin and blood vessels. Helps nosebleeds, aching bones, and backache.
Emotional/spiritual: good for meditation, grounding, and remote viewing. Helps grief, fear, anger, attachment, and neediness.

Melanite

A black variety of **andradite (garnet)**.

Common sources: Brazil, USA
Astrological association: Scorpio
Chakra: heart

Healing qualities

Physical: helps cancer, strokes, arthritis, rheumatism, and side-effects from medication.
Emotional/spiritual: helps jealousy, envy, distrust, anger, excess emotion, resentment, and animosity. Useful when you are going through divorce.

Merlinite

Black and white moss opal (opalite).

Common sources: India, USA
Astrological association: Pisces
Chakra: brow

Healing qualities

Good for seeing both sides of an argument, moving forward in life, optimism, and seizing the moment.
Physical: good for sexual energy and survival instincts.
Emotional/spiritual: calming. Good for all psychic abilities, yin/yang balance, flow, magic, and accessing the akashic records.

Obsidian

Volcanic glass that occurs in a variety of colors: **black**, brown, green, red/black, brown/black, **mahogany**, black with **rainbow** patterns/colors, silver or gold **sheen**, black and white **snowflake** patterns, blue, purple, translucent black and brown nodules (**apache tears**).

Common sources: Mexico, USA
Astrological associations:
Aries, Scorpio,
Sagittarius,
Capricorn
Chakra: base

Healing qualities

Brings wisdom and offers protection. Good for learning.
Physical: good for the colon, and male sexuality and qualities. Helps gastroenteritis, irritable bowel syndrome (IBS), wind pains, and nausea. Helps you recognize the causes of dis-ease.
Emotional/spiritual: grounding. Helps self-defeating patterns and subconscious blockages. Enables you to see your dark side. Integrates spirituality into everyday life. Aids access to roots and past experiences. Acts as a mirror of the soul – lets you take a long hard look at yourself, and then smile.

Black obsidian

Common sources: Mexico, USA
Astrological association: Sagittarius
Chakra: base

Healing qualities

Good for protection, creativity, male qualities, and intuition.
Physical: good for digestion and survival instincts.
Emotional/spiritual: grounding. Good for scrying (a form of divination), shamanic healing.

Sheen obsidian

Silver or gold sheen on black obsidian.

Common source: Mexico
Astrological association:
Sagittarius
Chakra: base

Healing qualities

Good for patience, change, and delays in your life plan.
Physical: tackles the sources of dis-ease.

Apache tear

Small translucent black or brown nodules.

Common source: USA
Astrological association: Aries
Chakra: base

Healing qualities

Good for change, moving forward in life, forgiveness, and spontaneity. Combats self-limiting beliefs.
Physical: good for the knees. Helps vitamin C and D deficiencies, muscle spasms, and snakebite. Aids detox.
Emotional/spiritual: good for emotions and emotional balance (helps you to shed tears, especially repressed tears). Helps behavior change, forgiveness, negativity, and grief.

Snowflake obsidian

Black **obsidian** with inclusions of white phenocryst.

Common source: USA
Astrological association:
Virgo
Chakra: base

Healing qualities
Good for bringing peace of mind. Encourages purity
(in all senses).
Physical: good for the stomach and sinuses (unblocks
the meridian linking these two areas). Good for veins,
bones, eyes and eyesight, and skin. Helps acalulia
(difficulty performing mathematical calculations).
Aids detox.
Emotional/spiritual: good for meditation. Helps anger,
resentment, unhelpful behavior patterns and loneliness.

Black opal

Forms black masses. Sometimes shows iridescence (fire)
in various colors.

Common sources: Australia,
Hungary, USA
Astrological associations:
Cancer, Scorpio,
Sagittarius
Chakra: base

**Healing
qualities**
Motivates you. Useful
in iridology.
Physical: good for eyesight, digestion, and fertility.
Emotional/spiritual: good for scrying (a form of
divination). Helps depression.

Picasso marble

Marble in color combinations of black, brown, yellow,
and white.

Common alternate names: Picasso stone, Picasso jasper
Common source: USA
Astrological associations:
Sagittarius, Cancer
Chakra: sacral

Healing qualities
Good for creativity, change, perseverance, and art.
Physical: good for metabolism, circulation, and
digestion. Helps carpal tunnel syndrome and weight
loss. Aids detox.
Emotional/spiritual: grounding and calming. Helps
subconscious or unsettled thoughts, stress, and anxiety.

Pyrolusite

Masses and dendrites in black, silver, gray, brown, or
blue.

Common sources: France, Germany
Astrological association: Leo
Chakra: sacral

Healing qualities
Good for change and
relationships.
Physical: good for the
sex drive, blood
vessels, eyes, and
metabolism.
Tackles the causes

of dis-ease. Helps bronchitis and wounds.
Emotional/spiritual: good for the aura. Helps negativity
and excess spiritual energy (a feeling that spirits won't
leave you alone).

Sphalerite

Occurs as masses, fibers, and cubic, tetrahedral, or dodecahedral crystals. May be colorless, black, brown, yellow, red, or green.

Common alternate name: blende
Common source: Mexico
Astrological association: Gemini
Chakra: solar plexus

Healing qualities

Good for protection, creativity, and career change.
Physical: good for blood flow, eyes, and nervous system. Helps anemia, weight gain, and nutrient absorption.
Emotional/spiritual: good for meditation, yin/yang balance, all psychic abilities, trance, and intuition (trust). Helps inferiority complex.

Tektite

Meteoritic glass created from the immense heat of a meteorite impact with the earth. The heat is so intense that both the meteorite and the earth's surface melt. As this mixture of space material and earth cool together, tektite is formed. May be black, brown, yellow Libyan glass or green **moldavite.**

Common sources: China, Thailand
Astrological associations: Aries, Cancer
Chakra: crown

Healing qualities

Good for abundance and reasoning.
Physical: good for circulation and fertility. Helps fever.
Emotional/spiritual: good for yin/yang balance, telepathy, psychic surgery, starting meditation, peak experiences during meditation, and also contact with other worlds.

Schorl

Black, vertically striated prismatic crystals.

Common alternate names: black **tourmaline**, afrisite
Common sources: Brazil, India, Pakistan
Astrological association: Capricorn
Chakra: base

Healing qualities

A "feel better" stone that is good for practicality, creativity, intellect, protection, and vitality. Helps clumsiness.
Physical: good for the heart and adrenal glands. Helps arthritis and dyslexia. Protects against radiation.
Emotional/spiritual: good for emotional stability and connection to the earth. Helps negativity, victim mentality, anxiety, and embarrassment.

Zebra rock

Quartz and basalt, with black and white stripes in a zebra pattern. The name zebra rock is given to at least three different mineral combinations: the one shown here; a schist from Australia; and a variety of marble known as black zebra/zebra stone from Pakistan.

Common source: USA
Astrological associations: Taurus, Gemini
Chakra: sacral

Healing qualities

Brings compassion.
Physical: good for teeth and gums. Helps dry skin, osteoporosis, bone cancer, muscle spasms, heart palpitations, and vitamin deficiencies. Gives access to reserves of energy, stamina, and endurance (good for athletes).
Emotional/spiritual: combats shallowness.

Gray banded agate

A gray and white banded or patterned variety of **agate**.

Common source:
Botswana
*Astrological
association:* Scorpio
Chakra: sacral

Healing qualities
Physical: good for the
release of stored energy. Helps fatigue, general malaise,
and myalgic encephalomyelitis (ME).

Flint

A variety of **chalcedony**. May be gray, black, or brown.

Common sources: worldwide
Astrological associations: Aries, Scorpio
Chakra: crown

Healing qualities
Brings physical protection. Helps you to read and
understand body language.
Physical: good for the liver, joints, lungs, and digestion.
Helps kidney stones, calcification of bones, skin
wounds, cuts, and superficial growths.

Emotional/spiritual: good
for telepathy, psychic
surgery, extra-sensory
perception (ESP), and
protecting houses from
spirits. Helps shyness, lack
of intimacy, arguments,
nightmares, and negativity.

Galena

Metallic silver/gray cubic and octahedral crystals. Also
found as masses, fibers, and unusual shapes.

Common source: UK
Astrological association:
Capricorn
Chakra: base

Healing qualities
Good for study (especially in the healing professions).
Physical: good for the hair, blood, veins, circulation,
and olfactory and nervous systems. Helps inflammation,
boils, and selenium and zinc deficiencies.
Emotional/spiritual: good for grounding and centering.
Helps self-limiting ideas/beliefs and anti-social
behavior.

Hematite

Occurs as masses, botryoidal forms, rosettes, layered
plates, and tabular and rhombohedral crystals. May be
metallic gray/silver, black, or brick red/brown.

Common sources: UK, Morocco
Astrological associations: Aries, Aquarius
Chakra: base

Healing qualities
Brings strength, love,
courage, and personal
magnetism. Good for
mental processes, thoughts,

memory, dexterity, and working with numbers/maths.
Physical: good for the spleen, blood, and vertebrae
(place one piece at the top and one piece at the base of
the spine). Helps anemia, backache, broken bones and
fractures, blood clots, air and travel sickness, jet lag,
insomnia, cramps, and myalgic encephalomyelitis (ME).

Pyrite

Occurs as cubic and dodecahedral crystals, occasionally flattened (pyrite suns) and masses. It becomes more golden with oxidation and may replace many minerals so can be found in other formations and in combination with other minerals.

Common alternate names: iron pyrites, fool's gold
Common sources: Peru, Spain, USA, UK
Astrological association: Leo
Chakras: solar plexus, all

Healing qualities

Good for the brain, memory, thought processes, "energy sparks", and leadership. Brings protection. Solves problems with pollution and noisy neighbors.
Physical: good for bones, lungs, cell formation, circulation, and digestion. Helps varicose veins, snoring, radiation sickness, bronchitis, infection, fever, and inflammation. Useful if you are accident prone.
Emotional/spiritual: helps negativity.

Marcasite

Chemically the same as **pyrite**, but the two stones are distinguished by their crystalline structures.

Common sources: Europe, USA
Astrological association: Leo
Chakras: solar plexus

Healing qualities

Physical: good for skin. Helps moles and warts.
Emotional/spiritual: helps ego, personality, and impatience.

Silver

Occurs as silver dendrites, scales, plates, nuggets, and, rarely, needle-like crystals. Oxidation causes the color to change to gray/black.

Common source: Mexico
Astrological associations: Cancer, Aquarius
Chakras: heart, throat, brow, crown

Healing qualities

Good for mental health and healing, and eloquence. Allows you to look into your heart to see who you really are. Helps a crude personality. Energizes other crystals (place silver near crystals during a full or new moon).
Physical: good for speech. Helps hepatitis, speech impediments, such as a stammer, and vitamin A and E deficiencies. Aids detox.
Emotional/spiritual: good for emotional balance, meditation, life cycles, astral travel, and distant/absent healing. Helps negativity.

Stibnite

Masses, columns, blades, and needle-like and prismatic crystals.

Common sources: Uzbekistan, China
Astrological associations: Scorpio, Capricorn
Chakra: crown

Healing qualities

Good for finding direction and making decisions. Assists teachers. Brings attractiveness, endurance, speed, money, and loyalty. Helps clingy relationships.
Physical: good for the stomach and esophagus. Helps stiffness.
Emotional/spiritual: good for meditation. Protects against evil spirits. Connects you to totem animals.

Brazilian agate

A translucent or transparent variety of **agate** with lines and patterns. May be brown, red, black, green, clear, white or gray. (Commonly dyed pink, purple, blue, or deep green.)

Common source: Brazil
Astrological association: Aries
Chakra: brow

Healing qualities

Brings protection.
Physical: good for the pulse rate. Helps minor injuries, such as bruises, sprains, and strains. Alleviates constipation.
Emotional/spiritual: good for dowsing, divination, visualization, astral travel, and shamanic contact with other worlds.

Crazy lace agate

A variety of **agate** with "crazy" patterns, bands, and wavy lines of cream, red, or brown.

Alternate name: Mexican lace agate
Common source: Mexico
Astrological associations: Gemini, Capricorn, Aquarius
Chakra: heart

Healing qualities

Brings confidence, balance, courage, self-esteem, and vitality.
Physical: good for the heart, skin, speech, and eyesight.
Emotional/spiritual: helps fear.

Turritella agate

A brown variety of **agate** found in masses with fossil inclusions.

Common source: USA
Astrological associations: Cancer, Aquarius
Chakra: base

Healing qualities

Good for change and survival instincts.
Physical: good for the absorption of food, especially trace elements. Helps fatigue, peristalsis, stomach upsets, bloating, and wind pains.
Emotional/spiritual: good for earth healing. Helps superiority complex and victim mentality.

Aragonite

Hexagonal column-shaped crystals (often linked to form "sputnik" shapes). Also found as fibers, masses, or stalactites. May be white, brown, yellow, blue, or green.

Common sources: Morocco, Namibia
Astrological association: Capricorn
Chakra: crown

Healing qualities

Good for problem-solving. Helps answers suddenly to become obvious. Encourages patience, practicality, and reliability.

Physical: good for the health of the skin. Helps general aches and pains, vitamins A and D deficiency, chills, hair loss, wrinkles, hard skin, and bunions. Alleviates stress-related skin conditions, such as eczema and psoriasis.

Emotional/spiritual: good for stilling the mind before meditation. Helps stress and anger.

Bronzite

Masses, fibers, and, rarely, crystals. Brown with gold flakes.

Common source: Brazil
Astrological association: Leo
Chakra: heart

Healing qualities

Gives you the courage to take your own path in life. Helps you make decisions.

Physical: good for pH balance, iron absorption, hemoglobin, and red blood cells. Helps anemia and cancer.

Emotional/spiritual: good for self-confidence.

Boji Stone®

Spherical or ovoid gray/brown stones with smooth patterns and/or protrusions. Mostly **pyrite** with some palladium and traces of various other minerals. Smooth stones are known as "female" stones; those with protrusions as "male". Stones are usually worked with in male/female pairs.

Common source: the Boji valley, Colorado, USA is the sole source (although other similar stones known as shaman stones or mochi marbles are available)
Astrological associations: Taurus, Leo, Scorpio, Aquarius
Chakra: base (one Boji stone), all other chakras (a male/female pair of Boji stones)

Healing qualities

Good for communication with animals.

Physical: helps tissue regeneration and pain. Speeds recovery.

Emotional/spiritual: good for energy, aura and grounding. When used in pairs, Boju stones align the body's energies and balance all the chakras. This energizes, centers, and grounds the body, mind, and spirit and feels like a rush of energy through the body. Helps energy blocks.

Chiastolite

A variety of andalusite forming fat crystals that exhibit a cross pattern in cross section. May be brown or green with black cross patterns.

Common alternate names: cross stone, andalusite
Common source: China
Astrological association: Libra
Chakra: sacral

Healing qualities

Good for devotion, change, problem-solving, creativity, and practicality. Helps you to be strong in difficult situations.

Physical: good for understanding death and the dying process. Helps fever, blood flow, milk in nursing mothers, and chromosome damage.

Emotional/spiritual: traditionally a sign of the Cross, associated with its healing energies. Good for re-birth and astral travel.

Fulgurite

Naturally fused **quartz** with various impurities giving brown shades of color. Formed from the effect of lightning strikes in deserts.

Common alternate names: petrified lightning, lechatelierite (a variety)
Common source: Libya
Astrological associations: Gemini, Virgo
Chakra: brow

Healing qualities

Good for communication and concentration.
Physical: good for the ears, nose, throat, esophagus, intestines, and colon.
Emotional/spiritual: good for psychic skills, especially dowsing.

Hessonite

A brown or cinnamon/yellow form of grossular **garnet**.

Common alternate name: cinnamon stone
Common source: Madagascar
Astrological association: Aries
Chakras: sacral, solar plexus

Healing qualities

Good for new challenges and courage.
Physical: good for the olfactory and lymphatic systems. Helps flatulence and colic. Aids detox.
Emotional/spiritual: good for meditation (helps you go to the next level). Helps with inferiority complex and negativity.

Picture jasper/picture stone

A tan or brown variety of **jasper**, with markings that suggest ancient pictures.

Common sources: USA, South Africa
Astrological association: Leo
Chakra: brow

Healing qualities

Allows you to see the bigger picture. Good for setting up your own business.
Physical: good for the immune system, kidneys, and skin.
Emotional/spiritual: good for creative visualization. Releases deep and hidden grief and fear.

Lingham

A brown/cream variety of **jasper** that is roughly the shape of a rugby ball.

Common alternate names: Shiva Lingham, Narmadeshvara Lingham
Common source: Ganges River and its tributaries, India
Astrological association: Scorpio
Chakras: all

Healing qualities

Physical: good for fertility, the spine, body fluids, and the prostate gland. Helps fluid retention, back pain, and menopause.
Emotional/spiritual: good for spiritual detox, connection to higher self, and reaching peak experiences in meditation. Helps to connects physical and spiritual energy. Enhances male energy.

Meteorite

Rocks from space that are commonly 4.5 billion years old (and up to 13 billion years old). They come from Mars, the Moon, the heads of comets, the asteroid belt and the debris of the "big bang". They are composed of minerals that are also found on earth; the difference is that, unlike earth minerals, space minerals don't have air gaps between molecules. This is because they are formed in the vacuum of space. Meteorites come in three classes: irons, chondrites, and achondrites. They are usually brown or black (possibly silver when polished). Other space material includes **tektite** and **moldavite**.

Common sources: Argentina, Russia, Namibia, China
Astrological associations: all
Chakras: crown, base

Healing qualities

Good for endurance. Assists spatial conception. Useful if you are emigrating.
Physical: iron meteorites help anemia.
Emotional/spiritual: good for meditation, connection with distant friends and loved ones, and contacting other worlds. Helps melancholy, incoherence, and home sickness.
No elixir with chondrites and achondrites.

Muscovite

A variety of mica usually forming layered "plates", "flowers", "books", scales and masses, and other crystalline forms. Colors include brown, green, pink, gray, violet, yellow, red, or white.

Common source: Brazil,
Astrological associations: Leo, Aquarius
Chakra: heart

Healing qualities

Good for speed of thought, problem-solving, and major life decisions. Useful if you are worried about the impact of your life situation on yourself and those who rely on you.
Physical: balances sleep patterns. Helps allergies, diabetes, hunger, dehydration, mononucleosis (glandular fever), and insomnia.
Emotional/spiritual: good for emotional expression, shamanic visions, and meditation. Helps you to listen to your intuition and access your higher self. Helps insecurity, self-doubt, pessimism, past issues, anger, tantrums, excess nervous energy, and painful emotions.

Mahogany obsidian

A brown/black variety of **obsidian**.

Common source: Mexico
Astrological association: Libra
Chakra: base

Healing qualities

Brings vitality and strength in times of need. Helps you to meet your goals.
Emotional/spiritual: help releases energy blocks. Helps ease tension.

Petrified wood

Fossilized trees in which the organic material has been replaced by one or more minerals; usually **agate**, **chalcedony**, or **quartz** (but many others may be present). Colors include brown, but can be any wood-like color or the colors of **agate**, **chalcedony**, and **opal**.

Common sources: USA, Madagascar
Astrological association: Leo
Chakra: base

Healing qualities

Good for longevity and mental balance. Combats pollution.
Physical: good for the bones. Helps arthritis, allergies, hayfever, and infection.
Emotional/spiritual: grounding. Soothes the emotions. Relieves stress. Helps access past lives.

Smoky quartz

Brown or black variety of **quartz** colored by natural radiation from the earth. This process can be duplicated in laboratories quite effectively – a lot of smoky quartz is man-made.

Common alternate names: smokey quartz, carnigorm
Common sources: Brazil, Madagascar, USA
Astrological associations: Sagittarius, Capricorn
Chakra: base

Healing qualities

Good for vitality, intuition, survival instincts, male energies, and mental activity. Offers protection by dissipating negativity (useful during ceremonies). Helpful if you habitually spend too much money. Helps you to move forward in life.
Physical: good for physical expression and sexual energy. Good for the legs, knees, ankles, hands, and feet. Helps stammering.
Emotional/spiritual: good for grounding, relaxation, sedation, meditation, and dream interpretation. Channels energy through the hands (for example, in reiki or spiritual healing). Helps with negativity, anger, depression, despair, and grief. Speeds up the laws of karma.

Rutile

Needle-like crystals often penetrating **quartz**, **rutilated quartz**, and prismatic crystals. Colors include bronze, silver, red, brown, red/brown, black, yellow, gold, and violet.

Common alternate name: angel hair
Common source: Brazil

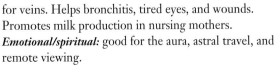

Astrological associations: Taurus, Gemini
Chakra: brow

Healing qualities

Good for sexuality and mental balance. Offers protection.
Physical: tackles the causes of dis-ease. Good for veins. Helps bronchitis, tired eyes, and wounds. Promotes milk production in nursing mothers.
Emotional/spiritual: good for the aura, astral travel, and remote viewing.

Sandstone

Stone composed of grains of sand. May be creamy/white, tan, or rusty-brown (sometimes blending into one another). Also found with beautiful rainbow-colored oxidations.

Common sources: India, UK, USA
Astrological association: Gemini
Chakra: sacral

Healing qualities

Good for creativity and relationships. Useful in groups. Aids clear thought. Helps those who are easily distracted.
Physical: good for eyesight and nails. Helps wounds, broken bones, water retention, and hair loss.
Emotional/spiritual: good for avoiding distractions during meditation. Helps moodiness and temper tantrums.

Septarian

Nodules of clay ironstone into which other minerals, such as **calcite**, **jasper**, **dolomite**, **aragonite**, and occasionally **barite**, are deposited through small cracks in the structure.

Common sources:
Australia,
Madagascar,
USA
*Astrological
association:* Taurus
Chakra: base

Healing qualities

Good for patience, endurance, and tolerance. Assists public speaking, sound therapy, and neuro-linguistic programming (NLP). Builds awareness of the environment.
Physical: good for physical flexibility. Good for the teeth, bones, and muscles. Helps melanoma.
Emotional/spiritual: good for emotional flexibility.

Staurolite

Short prismatic crystals with cruciform twinning that gives the shape of a cross.

*Common
alternative names:*
fairy cross, fairy stone
Common sources: France, Russia
Astrological association: Pisces
Chakra: base

Healing qualities

Brings good luck. Useful for rituals, protection, and time management.
Physical: helps fever and malaria. Useful during smoking cessation. Combats addictive personality traits.
Emotional/spiritual: helps stress and depression.

Dravite

A brown variety of **tourmaline.**

Common sources: Australia, Brazil, Europe, Nepal
Astrological association: Aries
Chakra: base

Healing qualities

Good for protection. Helps the environment.
Physical: good for the intestines. Helps spots and acne.
Emotional/spiritual: good for the aura and connection to the earth.

Chapter 4
Crystal Remedies

Understanding ailments

Health is a balance of physical, mental, emotional, and spiritual energies. These energies are both within us and exist around us. The energies around us are created by our interaction with, and our experience of, the world. How we are within ourselves both creates and reflects the energies around us. In this way, we are inescapably linked to our surroundings. The Buddhist view of emptiness, scientific theories such as Einstein's theory of relativity, and Feynman's work in quantum electrodynamics and quantum field theory all agree that each of us is connected to everything. The idea that anything can exist by itself is simply illusion. Every single action is the result of another, and gives rise to more.

Balancing energies

When our energies are balanced, we are in a state of wellbeing. When they are unbalanced, we are in a state of "dis-ease" and we become increasingly susceptible to all kinds of illness. The term "dis-ease" rather than "disease" is employed throughout this book in order to emphasize imbalance, in that the word shows us that illness means being out of kilter with ourselves. Angelite, blue lace agate, calcite (all varieties), carnelian, crazy lace agate, emerald, jade, opal, quartz crystal, ruby, rutilated quartz, silver, tiger's eye, and tourmaline all help in different ways to balance out our energies, removing dis-ease and maintaining or restoring health in the process.

Any stress, whether it is emotional, mental, or spiritual, may result in the manifestation of physical symptoms of an illness. This is not the same as psychosomatic illness, in that the illness is real. The physical body may be weakened, often by years of stress. Amethyst, carnelian, obsidian, pyrolusite, rhyolite, rutile, sheen obsidian, sugilite, ulexite, and unakite can help you recognize, understand, and therefore alter the underlying situations that give rise to stress.

Long-term emotional strain can sometimes, unfortunately, become a natural part of life. In order to cope with it, you start to accept or ignore it. Once this happens it is often difficult to change your behavioral patterns. The crystals listed above can help you recognize the underlying cause of dis-ease. The underlying cause may also be tackled by working with crystals on any manifesting symptoms (see Physical Ailments, pages 107–123).

Within this chapter are more than 250 crystal remedies for common ailments. First are Physical Ailments followed by Emotional Ailments, with recommended crystal prescriptions for each condition listed. They are presented separately for ease of reference, as many physical symptoms, as explained above, can have an emotional cause. The second section is concerned with enhancement – Crystals for Spiritual Enhancement and Crystals for Life Enhancement. Here you will find crystals to further aid your self-development, from stones for psychic protection to those that help your communication with animals or further inspire your creative soul.

Below left, clockwise, from top
Polished purple fluorite, raw apatite (x3), polished citrine, polished tiger's eye (center), polished amber (below left), and polished carnelian.

Above
Polished tiger's eye and a citrine point (left).

Remedies for physical ailments

Crystals work by balancing our subtle energies (also known as chi, prana, or universal life force energy). As these energies slowly find a point of equilibrium, our state of wellbeing improves. The symptoms of any ailments reduce or go away completely.

All physical ailments have an underlying cause, and crystals will tackle this cause directly. A physical symptom may be the result of many different underlying causes so, if you do not find a benefit from one crystal, try another. I have often listed several crystals for a single ailment. Try the crystal(s) in **bold** first. If you have no reaction at all after 30 minutes, try one of the alternatives or look for another description of your ailment. If in doubt, try **quartz crystal**, azeztulite, epidote, phenacite, or sugilite, as these are often helpful for any condition. Purple fluorite helps most dis-ease on a deep spiritual level, while an elixir of shattuckite can be beneficial in the treatment of all minor illnesses. Gem silica will enhance other crystal remedies. Where a + sign appears in an ailment entry, the crystals should be worked with in combination. The more you work with the same crystal(s) for the same condition, the quicker and more effective it or they will be.

Because crystals are moving your energies, you can sometimes feel worse before you feel better. Don't worry about this; it usually lasts only a few minutes, although in some cases it can last for up to 21 days. Crystals can cleanse or detox the chakra system and, as this happens, you may find that your physical symptoms change and move around your body. This is because crystals unearth deep issues inside you which you do not want to face. If you allow this process to happen, you will feel unbelievably better at the end.

In my own and many others' experience, a full course of crystal healing leads to an improvment in a client's state of wellbeing. You should be aware that symptoms are always an expression of an underlying illness or dis-ease. Therefore, if you feel unwell, you are strongly advised to seek advice from a qualified medical or alternative practitioner of your choice. Although science has proved that crystals do many things, there is, to date, no experimental evidence that any crystal has a direct effect on any physical ailment in the human body.

ABDOMINAL COLIC Hold a **citrine** crystal or white coral to the worst point of the pain for 30 minutes. Carry or wear citrine to reduce or prevent further attacks.

ABDOMINAL DISTENSION Hold idocrase to the affected area.

ABSCESS Hold **amethyst** to the abscess or apply a jade elixir topically.

ACHILLES TENDON, INJURY TO Hold **dumortierite** or magnesite to the tendon.

ACHING MUSCLES Hold an **aventurine** stone to the aching muscle for at least 30 minutes. Carry rose quartz or charoite with you during the day. An aragonite elixir can also help. If symptoms persist, tape a piece of lodestone to the muscle.

ACID INDIGESTION Hold bornite, dolomite or **peridot** to your chest just above the area of discomfort. As indigestion lowers, move the crystal down accordingly until the discomfort has gone. Carry or wear peridot to reduce or prevent recurrence.

ACIDITY, EXCESS Carry or wear dolomite or **peridot**.

ACIDOSIS Carry or wear peridot.

ACNE Carry or wear any of the following crystals (or keep a larger crystal by your bed or anywhere you spend a lot of time): **amethyst**, amber, dravite, jade, or selenite. Hold one of these crystals to the worst spot each day. You can also make an elixir from **amber** and apply it to your skin.

ADDICTION Kunzite is excellent for acute addictions, **lepidolite** for milder cases and **blue chalcedony** for those linked to childhood issues. Amethyst can help with withdrawal symptoms. **Blue chalcedony + brecciated jasper + lepidolite + peridot + topaz**, smithsonite or zeolite can help alcoholics. **Lepidolite** or staurolite can set you free from your addictive personality. Barite speeds a return to normality after the addiction is broken.

ADRENAL GLAND DISORDERS To treat problems such as Cushing's syndrome and hyperaldosteronism, hold a piece of **sugilite** for at least 30 minutes each day. Dolomite, nephrite, rose quartz and schorl, or an aventurine elixir may also be helpful.

AIDS (ACQUIRED IMMUNE DEFICIENCY SYNDROME) Treatment for AIDS must be on a daily basis, with a trained crystal therapist if possible. **Chevron amethyst**, nebula stone, petalite, schalenblende, and titanium quartz are helpful. Dioptase can help to increase your T-cell count. See also **IMMUNE SYSTEM** and the individual symptoms of active AIDS-related conditions.

AIR SICKNESS Carry hematite + turquoise. Play with them to get as much skin contact as you can.

ALLERGIES Carry or wear cleavelandite, muscovite, petrified wood, topaz, **turquoise** or zircon for the prevention and treatment of allergies. A **spirit quartz** elixir is good for skin allergies. **Chlorite** is helpful for the immediate relief of the symptoms of allergic reactions.

ALOPECIA Hold petalite to affected areas.

ALZHEIMER'S DISEASE Carry or wear cerussite or **alexandrite**. Amber and rhodochrosite are helpful aids to memory.

ANEMIA Carry or wear bloodstone, bornite, bronzite, citrine, **garnet**, goethite, hematite, meteorite, prehnite, ruby, sphalerite, or tiger iron 24 hours a day. Continue for at least three months after the condition improves to prevent relapse.

ANAL DISCOMFORT (as a result of hemorrhoids, minor infections or inflammatory conditions, such as Crohn's disease) Place a piece of **citrine**, tiger's eye or falcon's eye beneath a cushion or pillow on your seat.

FOR HEALTHY BONES

For bone health, work with the following crystals (carry or wear them, hold them to relevant areas and/or place a larger crystal in your immediate vicinity): amethyst, azurite/malachite, coral, dolomite, emerald, **fluorite**, garnet, howlite, jade, lapis lazuli, magnesite, magnetite, **petrified wood**, purple fluorite, pyrite, rhodonite, scapolite, snowflake obsidian, or zircon. Gypsum and **septarian** (as an elixir) strengthen weakened bones.

ANAPHYLACTIC SHOCK Moonstone speeds recovery after the incident is under control.

ANGINA Carry or wear bornite, **dioptase** or emerald. Place a large piece by your bed, on your desk or in a place where you spend a lot of time. Carry or wear magnesite to improve the health of the cardiac arteries.

ANKLE, DISCOMFORT Hold smoky quartz to the affected ankle.

ANKLES, WEAK Hold smoky quartz to ankles.

ANOREXIA Carry or wear carnelian or **fluorite**. Meditate with **fluorite** daily (see chapter 2) and hold a piece before meals.

APPETITE Carnelian increases and apatite decreases appetite.

ARC (AIDS-RELATED COMPLEX) See **AIDS** and specific symptoms.

ARTERIOSCLEROSIS Hold **cleavelandite** or magnesite to affected areas.

ARTHRITIS Hold the following crystals to the worst affected joint for at least 30 minutes each day: apatite, azurite, blue lace agate, chalcanthite, **chrysocolla + copper**, garnet, gold, lodestone, malachite, melanite, petrified wood, rhodonite, schorl, or turquoise. You may find that as one joint improves another will become worse. An amethyst elixir may also relieve chronic symptoms.

ASTHMA The following crystals alleviate asthma symptoms: amber, amethyst, azurite/malachite, carnelian, chrysocolla, cleavelandite, jade, malachite, morganite, rose quartz, and vanadinite. Carry or wear **turquoise** if your asthma results from pollen allergy. Carry or wear **emerald** if your asthma is genetic and not exacerbated by pollen.

ASTIGMATISM Place peridot on the eyelid.

ASTRINGENT Gently rub a sapphire crystal against your skin for a few seconds to help close the pores.

ATTENTION DEFICIT DISORDERS ADD/ADHA/ADHD Wear **charoite** and goshenite and keep them near your bed at night. Holding **blue calcite** can help immediate symptoms.

AUTISM Carry or wear **charoite**, gold, **goshenite,** or **sodalite**. Place under pillow or next to bed at night.

BACK PAIN Trapped, compressed or swollen nerves can cause severe pain. Lie down and place carnelian, fuchsite, garnet, gold, lingham, quartz crystal, **selenite,** or sunstone on or under your back. Carry or wear these crystals for chronic conditions.

BACKACHE Lie on your front with a long piece of **selenite** on your spine, or put the crystal under your mattress at night. Carry fluorite, hematite, jasper, lapis lazuli, lingham, magnetite, sapphire, or turquoise. **Aventurine** or topaz will help if pain is due to muscle damage. Use **fluorite** for lower backache (lumbago).

BACTERIAL INFECTION Carry, wear or hold to affected area: amber, **amethyst**, emerald, jade, or nephrite. See also specific symptoms of infection.

BALANCE, PROBLEMS WITH Amethyst, angelite, apatite, bloodstone, Boji stones (a pair), carnelian, dioptase, emerald, jade, malachite, moldavite, orange calcite, **quartz crystal**, ruby, rutilated quartz, sodalite, tiger's eye, and tourmaline can all help. Hold one of these whilst sitting quietly for 30 minutes each day until balance improves.

BELCHING Carry or wear beryl.

BELL'S PALSY To alleviate symptoms, hold aventurine + garnet + zircon to the affected area for 5–10 minutes several times a day. Carry these crystals with you all day and place them under your pillow or next to your bed at night.

BILE DUCT DISORDERS To treat problems such as bile duct strictures, carry or wear **emerald** or jasper. Hold to the skin above the liver for at least 30 minutes each day.

BILIOUSNESS Hold **emerald** or pearl.

BITES, INSECT Hold emerald, moonstone, or **sulfur** to the affected area.

BITES, VENOMOUS Hold **chalcedony** or sulfur to the affected area.

BLADDER PROBLEMS To treat infections or incontinence, carry or wear **amber**, jade, jasper, prehnite, tourmaline, or vanadinite. You can also tape a small piece on your skin. Work with **uvarovite** if you have a bladder infection.

BLOATING Hold chlorite, pearl, **turritella agate,** or zeolite to your abdomen.

BLOOD CIRCULATION/FLOW To improve circulation carry or wear amethyst, agate, azurite/malachite, bloodstone, chiastolite, chlorite, copper, coral, dioptase, galena, **garnet**, gold, golden ray calcite, lepidolite, moonstone, okenite, opal, Picasso marble, pyrite, rhodochrosite, rose quartz, ruby, sphalerite, tektite, turquoise, or variscite.

BLOOD CLEANSING/DETOXIFICATION Carry or wear these crystals over your heart: **amethyst**, copper, garnet, jade, ruby, or tourmaline.

BLOOD CLOTTING/BLEEDING (MINOR) Hold bloodstone, ruby, sapphire, or **shattuckite** to the site of the wound.

BLOOD DISORDERS Carry or wear any combination of these crystals (choose the ones that you are drawn to): **almandine**, aquamarine, bloodstone, blue quartz, cavansite, chrysocolla, cinnabar, galena, gold, **hematite**, malachite, rose quartz, and tiger iron.

BLOOD PRESSURE Carry or wear **dioptase** or pietersite for fluctuations in blood pressure. Carry or wear garnet, **ruby,** or tourmaline for low blood pressure. Carry or wear chrysocolla, chrysoprase, emerald, jade, jadeite, kunzite, or **sodalite** for high blood pressure.

BLOOD SUGAR LEVELS, IMBALANCE Carry or wear chrysocolla.

BODY ODOR (BO) Carry or wear **magnesite** or sunstone to neutralize personal odor.

Make crystal elixirs with water and drink or apply to the skin. Check the safety of any crystal for using in an elixir before you do so – see the Crystal Finder, pages 32–103).

BOILS Hold galena or **sapphire** to the affected area or drink okenite elixir.

BONE CANCER Carry or wear calcite, **peridot**, titanium quartz, and zebra rock all the time. In addition, hold them to any areas of discomfort.

BONE MARROW DISEASES Carry or wear bloodstone, chalcedony, erythrite, lapis lazuli, onyx, or purple fluorite. **Garnet** is associated with regenerating the blood, encouraging the production of more red blood cells. Carry or wear it.

BONES, GENERAL ACHES Hold **magnetite** or rose quartz to the affected areas.

BRAIN, INJURY OR DAMAGE Hold aquamarine, epidote, indicolite, kyanite, pyrite, ruby, tiger's eye, or **verdelite** to the head.

BREAST DISORDERS For non-cancerous lumps and fibrocystic breast disease, hold **okenite** to the required area.

BREATHING, TO EASE Wear a pendant or hold chrysocolla or **turquoise**. Vanadinite can also aid breath control.

BRONCHITIS Wear a pendant of carnelian, chalcopyrite, **chrysocolla**, jasper, nebula stone, pyrite, pyrolusite, rutile, tourmaline, or turquoise.

BRUISING Hold angelite, **fluorite**, gold, magnetite, pyrolusite, or rubellite to bruised areas.

BULIMIA Carry or wear fluorite and hold one hour before meals.

BUNIONS Hold **apatite** or aragonite to the affected area.

BURNS For mild burns hold **rose quartz** to the affected area. For severe burns place it near the area but not in contact with damaged tissue.

BURSITIS Hold copper to the affected joint. In extreme cases, tape it to the joint.

CALCIUM DEFICIENCY Carry or wear **calcite**, chlorite, garnet, septarian, sodalite, stilbite, or thulite.

CALMING, PHYSICAL Hold orange calcite.

CANCER Carry or wear **amethyst + carnelian + citrine**, azeztulite, bronzite, covellite, dolomite, melanite, **peridot**, **petalite**, selenite, or **sugilite**. Hold to any areas of discomfort for as long as possible and as many times as needed each day. You can also tape crystals to relevant areas. Malachite can help with non-malignant tumors. Fluorite can help in the early stages of disease.

CARPAL TUNNEL SYNDROME Hold fuchsite or **Picasso marble** to the wrist for a minimum of 30 minutes daily.

CARTILAGE, INJURY TO Hold dalmatian stone, **larimar** or sunstone to the affected joint for a minimum of 30 minutes daily. This can also relieve pain.

CATARACTS Bathe the eye in **abalone shell** elixir or hold **scapolite** or turquoise to the closed eye.

Place pyrite under your pillow to reduce snoring.

CELLULITIS Apply an elixir of green moss agate.

CENTRAL NERVOUS SYSTEM, DYSFUNCTION Carry or wear fire opal.

CHEMOTHERAPY, SIDE EFFECTS Carry, wear or keep chalcopyrite near your bed.

CHEST CONDITIONS See **HEART, LUNGS,** and **SPLEEN**

CHILBLAINS Hold gold to the affected areas.

CHOLERA Hold **malachite** or place it next to your bed. Carry or wear **opal** to protect yourself from the disease.

CHOLESTEROL, IMBALANCE Carry or wear bowenite, chalcanthite, **chrysoberyl**, magnesite, or yellow fluorite to balance the different types of cholesterol in the blood.

CHRONIC FATIGUE SYNDROME (CFS) Carry or wear petalite, **rhodochrosite + rhodonite + topaz**.

COLIC Hold **hessonite** or **nephrite** to the area of discomfort.

COLITIS Carry or wear **agate + citrine + obsidian + peridot + tiger's eye** or green fluorite, and hold to areas of discomfort until the discomfort eases.

COLON DISORDERS Carry or wear **agate**, fulgurite, green fluorite, halite, obsidian, or peridot. Hold to any areas of discomfort.

COMMON COLD Carry or wear **carnelian**, fluorite, green opal, jet, or **topaz**. Green moss agate can also help symptoms.

COMPLEXION, DULL Carry or wear aventurine or **rose quartz**, or wash your face with a rose quartz elixir. Carry or wear **almandine** or garnet.

CONNECTIVE TISSUE DISORDERS Carry or wear **prehnite** or pink opal.

CONSTIPATION Leave **amber** to stand in a glass of water for one hour and then drink the elixir. Hold Brazilian agate, lepidolite, moonstone, or **verdelite** to the abdomen (or wear them for chronic constipation).

CONVULSIONS Carry or wear **goethite** or magnesite all the time to reduce occurrences.

COOLING (IN A HOT CLIMATE) Carry or wear aquamarine and hold when necessary.

COORDINATION Carry or wear gold and hold for a few minutes before attempting complicated tasks.

CORNS Soak the feet in a warmed marcasite elixir.

COUGH Carry or wear rose quartz.

CRAMP Carry or wear aventurine, dalmatian stone, **hematite**, jadeite, jasper, lepidolite, or **lodestone**. Also hold to affected muscles. **Chrysocolla** can be effective for cramp in the arms and legs.

CRITICAL CONDITIONS Clinochlore can stabilize you and should be applied as necessary in each case.

CROHN'S DISEASE Carry or wear **aventurine + carnelian + chrysocolla + citrine + green moss agate + hawk's eye + peridot + tourmaline** all the time. Hold to any areas of discomfort.

CUTS AND GRAZES Hold **jasper** to the injury, or apply a **carnelian** elixir to the skin.

CYSTITIS Carry or wear **jade** or **uvarovite**. Hold to any areas of discomfort, such as the abdominal or kidney region.

DEAFNESS Carry or wear lapis lazuli.

DEHYDRATION Hold epidote, **green moss agate**, muscovite, or titanium quartz. Keep crystals around you until you have recovered.

DERMATITIS Hold wavellite to affected areas of skin.

DEXTERITY Hold chrysoprase, hematite, or **smoky quartz** each day for 20–30 minutes.

DIABETES Carry or wear chrysocolla, muscovite, opal, pink opal, **quartz crystal + sodalite**, rainforest rhyolite, or serpentine all the time.

DIARRHEA Carry or wear **aventurine + hawk's eye** or dioptase. Okenite is helpful in mild cases.

DIGESTIVE SYSTEM AND DIGESTIVE PROBLEMS
Citrine, goethite, rubellite and tiger's eye are useful in the treatment of any digestive problem. Carry or wear the crystal or hold it to the affected area to relieve discomfort. Black obsidian, black opal, carnelian, chrysocolla, **citrine**, coral, flint, gold, green moss agate, labradorite, lapis lazuli, lepidolite, opal, orbicular jasper, pearl, peridot, Picasso marble, pietersite, pyrite, smithsonite, tiger's eye, tourmaline, or yellow jasper can also be helpful.

DISCOMFORT Move a **quartz crystal** point clockwise over the affected area until the discomfort has gone. Or hold **sugilite** in your hand and focus your mind on the area of discomfort.

DIVERTICULITIS Carry or wear idocrase or **tiger's eye**. Hold to the area of discomfort and pain as often and as long as needed.

DIZZINESS Hold dioptase or **lapis lazuli** until symptoms stop.

DNA/RNA Ametrine, bowenite, chalcopyrite, herkimer diamond, and **leopard skin rhyolite** all stimulate replication which is required for healing and growth.

DRUNKENNESS Carry or wear amethyst when consuming alcohol – this can slow the effects of alcohol and reduces the tendency to drink too much.

DUCTLESS GLAND DISORDERS (For example, diabetes.) Carry or wear adamite.

DYSLEXIA Carry or wear gold, scapolite, schorl, or **sugilite**.

EAR, INNER, DISORDERS (Ménière's disease, deafness, dizziness and vertigo.) Hold blue fluorite against the ear.

EARACHE Slowly move a quartz crystal point in small clockwise circles near the ear until the discomfort goes away.

EATING DISORDERS Hold carnelian or **fluorite** for one hour before eating. Keep them on the table while you eat. Over a few weeks your eating pattern will begin to return to normal.

ECZEMA Hold **fuchsite**, kyanite, or selenite to the worst affected area for 30 minutes each day. Don't be concerned that one area will get better while another gets worse – just pick the worst spot each day. After two weeks the condition should have noticeably improved. Also try an aragonite elixir.

EMPHYSEMA Carry, wear, or tape chrysocolla, fire opal, **labradorite**, morganite, or rhodonite to chest.

ENDOCRINE GLANDS, DISORDERS Hold **amethyst**, golden ray calcite, or pietersite to relevant area and carry or wear during the day. Amber, amethyst, **blue quartz,** or sapphire are helpful for the whole endocrine system. Place them on your bedside table at night.

ENDOMETRIOSIS Carry, wear, or hold jade to areas of pain or discomfort.

ENDURANCE (PHYSICAL) Carry or wear halite, magnetite, malachite, meteorite, septarian, sodalite, or **stibnite**. Place zebra rock in areas where athletes train.

ENERGY BLOCKS (CAUSING PHYSICAL DIS-EASE) Place boji stone, **kyanite**, mahogany obsidian, or rhodolite on the area of the body where you feel the block is for 30–60 minutes. Your placement may relate to physical symptoms or simply be intuitive. Carry the crystal with you and repeat daily. You will notice when the block has cleared. Physical symptoms may clear up or you may feel re-energized or calm and peaceful. Fuchsite, rhodolite, serpentine, and **wavellite** can also increase energy flow. You can also carry or wear chalcopyrite or **kunzite** and hold to the area of the energy block (if you know where it is).

ENERGY EXCESS Hold fluorite, orange calcite, or **red calcite** (carry or wear them for longer-term relief).

ENERGY, PHYSICAL Carry or wear almandine, bornite, **carnelian**, citrine, diamond, gold, golden ray calcite, quartz crystal, ruby, rutilated quartz, smoky quartz, spinel, sulfur, sunstone, topaz, or yellow jasper.

EPILEPSY Carry or wear **malachite + sugilite** all the time. Also try bornite, gold, jet, and selenite.

ERYTHEMA Hold **gold** or selenite to the affected area for 20–30 minutes several times each day until the redness goes. Repeat daily for at least one week after symptoms abate.

ESOPHAGEAL PROBLEMS To treat problems such as Crohn's disease or esophageal pain, carry or wear citrine, fulgurite, **indicolite**, stibnite, or tiger's eye, and hold to any painful area.

EUSTACHIAN TUBE, BLOCKAGES (Caused by colds, sinus blockage, and altitude changes, such as air travel.) Hold lapis lazuli behind the ear for 10 minutes. Repeat often and as required.

EXHAUSTION Hold aragonite, **copper**, tanzanite, or vanadinite, or carry or wear for chronic symptoms.

EYE DISEASE Place tiger's eye on the eyelids for 10 minutes several times each day.

EYE DISORDERS Place eudialyte, green moss agate, **jade**, or scapolite on the eyelids for 15–30 minutes and repeat until symptoms abate. You can use all of the following crystals in the same way to aid the eyes: abalone shell, almandine, aquamarine, cavansite, celestite, charoite, chevron amethyst, clear fluorite, covellite, **fire agate**, gold, green moss agate, indicolite, labradorite, moonstone, opal, pyrolusite, scapolite, sphalerite, **tanzanite**, ulexite, or verdelite. A snowflake obsidian elixir may also help.

EYE STRAIN Place aventurine + fire agate on the eyelids.

EYELID DISORDERS (For example, blepharitis). Hold petalite to the eyelid.

EYES, SORE Place clear fluorite on the eyelids.

EYES, TIRED Bathe the eyes in **blue lace agate** elixir or place rutile on the eyelids.

EYESIGHT, POOR Hold agate, apophyllite, aquamarine, barite, black opal, blue lace agate, boulder opal, citrine, clear fluorite, crazy lace agate, diamond, emerald, malachite, **fire agate**, **fire opal,** or opal to the eyelids. Bathe the eyes in snowflake obsidian elixir.

FATIGUE AND TIREDNESS Carry or wear blue opal, **gray banded agate**, or turritella agate. Energy can be restored by holding **turritella agate**. Carry it with you, especially when driving through the night.

FEET, SORE Hold **larimar**, onyx, or smoky quartz to affected areas. Sunstone relieves aching feet.

FERTILITY, BOOSTING Carry or wear black opal, bowenite, chrysoprase, cinnabar, emerald, gypsum, jade, lingham, **moonstone**, pearl, **rose quartz**, spirit quartz, tektite, or unakite, and hold to belly for at least 10 minutes each evening. Meditate with grossularite.

FEVER Hold or place any of these crystals next to your bed: **aquamarine**, bornite, Brazilianite, chalcopyrite, chiastolite, green opal, iolite, magnesite, okenite, opal, pietersite, pyrite, ruby, sphene, staurolite, tektite, or titanium quartz. Drink hematite elixir.

FIBROIDS Hold jade + aventurine + sulfur to the area of the womb daily for 30 minutes, and carry or wear ruby.

FIBROMYALGIA Carry or wear **abalone shell + amethyst + selenite + rutilated quartz** and hold to any areas of infection or discomfort.

FIBROSITIS Place **aventurine** or selenite under your mattress at night.

FIBROUS TISSUE GROWTHS Hold sulfur to affected area.

FLATULENCE Carry or wear hessonite, thulite, or **tiger's eye**.

FLU Carry or wear fluorite, green opal, **jasper**, rose quartz, or **turquoise**. Hold green moss agate to relieve symptoms.

FLUID RETENTION Carry or wear **aquamarine**, blue lace agate, or lingham and hold to areas of swelling.

FOOD POISONING, PREVENTION Carry or wear citrine when eating out.

FRACTURE Hold blue lace agate, **chrysocolla + copper**, hematite, or lapis lazuli to the damaged bone. You can also tape crystals in place.

FREE RADICALS To combat damage to the body by free radicals, carry or wear **selenite**, and place **chalcanthite** in your immediate vicinity.

FRIGIDITY Uvarovite relaxes social and sexual barriers.

FROZEN SHOULDER Hold azurite/malachite in the hand on the side of the affected shoulder.

Chrysocolla can help muscle aches and stiffness.

FUNGAL INFECTION Carry or wear green moss agate.

GALLBLADDER DISORDERS (For example, gallstones.) Carry or wear azurite/malachite, carnelian, **citrine**, danburite, golden ray calcite, herderite, imperial topaz, jade, jasper, peridot, or **tsilasite**.

GALLSTONES Hold peridot to area of discomfort.

GASTROENTERITIS Place agate, **citrine**, obsidian, peridot, tiger's eye, or topaz near bed. Hold to areas of discomfort as required.

GERMAN MEASLES/RUBELLA Place an amethyst cluster next to your bed.

GLANDULAR FEVER Carry or wear sapphire or place next to bed.

GLAUCOMA Place scapolite on eyelid for short periods. Repeat often.

GOITRE Hold zeolite to the front of the neck for a minimum of 20–30 minutes daily. Repeat as often as desired.

GOOD BACTERIA, PROMOTION/STIMULATION Carry or wear chlorite.

GOUT Hold **bornite** or prehnite to affected joints.

GUM DISEASE Gently hold coral, **fluorite**, pyromorphite, or zebra rock to affected areas.

HEMOGLOBIN, DISORDERS (For example, thalassemia(s) and sickle cell anemia.) Carry or wear angelite or **bronzite.**

HEMOPHILIA Carry or wear shattuckite.

HEMORRHAGE Hold **bloodstone** or ruby to area.

HEMORRHOIDS Place **citrine** or tiger's eye beneath a cushion or pillow on your seat.

HAIR, DULL Carry or wear **aragonite**, **blue opal**, larimar, magnetite, petrified wood, or zincite. Massage a jade elixir or moonstone elixir into the scalp. **Chalcopyrite** promotes hair growth.

HAIR LOSS Carry or wear aragonite, blue opal, galena, sandstone, or **selenite**.

HAY FEVER Carry or wear petrified wood or **turquoise**. Carnelian can help with symptoms.

HEADACHE Hold **amethyst** or sugilite to the pain.

HEARING DIFFICULTIES Carry or wear amethyst, celestite, lapis lazuli, or **quartz crystal**.

HEART PALPITATIONS Hold zebra rock.

HEART PROBLEMS Many crystals are associated with helping the action of the heart, such as improving auricular and ventricular muscle function and regulating erratic heartbeat. Carry, wear or hold the crystal. Lie down and place the crystal on the center of your chest. Try any of the following: adamite, almandine, amazonite, amber, amethyst, anyolite, aventurine, azurite/malachite, bloodstone, bowenite, citrine, charoite, chrysoprase, crazy lace agate, dioptase, elbaite, emerald, fuchsite, garnet, gold, jade, kunzite, lepidolite, lime green tourmaline, **malachite**, peridot, pink opal, quartz crystal, rhodochrosite, rhodolite, rhodonite, rose quartz, rubellite, ruby, sapphire, schorl, unakite, uvarovite, verdelite, watermelon tourmaline, or zoisite. Drink a Brazilian agate elixir daily.

HEATSTROKE Hold brazilianite.

HEMERALOPIA Carry or wear abalone shell during the day. Place on the eyelids for 15–20 minutes first thing in the morning.

HEPATITIS Carry or wear silver.

Wearing crystal jewelry harnesses the healing qualities of your chosen stones.

HERNIA Hold or place aventurine, mookaite, or **lapis lazuli** on the area for 30 minutes daily.

HERPES Carry or wear fluorite or **nebular stone**.

HIP, DISCOMFORT Hold or tape bloodstone or **chrysocolla** to the point of discomfort.

HIV (HUMAN IMMUNO-DEFICIENCY VIRUS) Carry or wear chevron amethyst.

HORMONE HYPOSECRETION AND HYPERSECRETION Carry or wear kunzite.

HORMONE IMBALANCE Carry or wear amber, **amethyst**, gold, imperial topaz, or sapphire. Cassiterite and elbaite can help to balance hormone levels. Amethyst and **moonstone** can be particularly helpful for female hormone imbalance.

HUNGER Hold muscovite.

HYPERACTIVITY Hold two orange calcite stones, one in each hand, to restore energy balance.

HYPOGLYCEMIA Carry or wear pink opal or **rainforest rhyolite**. Place **serpentine** next to your bed.

HYPOTENSION See **BLOOD PRESSURE** (low).

HYPOTHERMIA Hold **gold**, green opal, magnesite, or pietersite.

IBS (IRRITABLE BOWEL SYNDROME) Carry, wear and hold to areas of discomfort: **citrine + dioptase + green moss agate + obsidian + peridot + hawk's eye**, or agate.

IMMUNE SYSTEM CLEANSING Place green moss agate next to your bed at night.

IMMUNITY Carry or wear ruby.

IMMUNODEFICIENCY DISORDERS Carry or wear **amethyst**, emerald, green opal, **howlite**, jade, lapis lazuli, malachite, nephrite, picture jasper, ruby, rutilated quartz, schalenblende, smithsonite, sphene, or verdelite. Place any of these around your home and workplace.

IMPOTENCY Carry or wear variscite. Sit mindfully holding the crystal for 30 minutes each day.

INCONTINENCE Carry or wear scapolite.

INDIGESTION Hold aventurine + hawk's eye, **citrine** or peridot to the area of discomfort.

INFECTED WOUND Hold copper to the wound.

INFECTION Carry or wear **amethyst**, **carnelian**, emerald, green calcite, jade, opal, petrified wood, pyrite, sapphire, or sulfur. Hold to the site of external infections for 30 minutes and repeat every few hours. **Sulfur** is particularly good for this. **Golden ray calcite** can be effective at the start of infections and **fluorite** can be helpful for severe infections.

INFECTION, INTERNAL Carry or wear chrysoberyl.

INFECTION, PREVENTION Carry or wear green calcite.

INFECTIOUS DISEASE Keep angelite or **chevron amethyst** near your bed.

INFERTILITY Place selenite next to your bed.

INFIRMITY Carry or wear elbaite.

INFLAMMATION Hold chalcopyrite, **emerald**, erythrite, galena, malachite, or pyrite to the site of inflammation.

INFLAMMATION, JOINTS Hold copper to the affected joint for 30-minute sessions as and when required.

INSECT REPELLENT Apply an elixir of angelite to the skin.

INSOMNIA Hold **malachite** one hour before you want to go to sleep and keep holding the crystal when you go to bed. Your sleep pattern will improve the first night and should return to normal after two weeks. Larvakite, muscovite, and strawberry quartz also enhance restful sleep. Carrying or wearing amethyst, cerussite, hematite, lapis lazuli, manganoan calcite, muscovite, sodalite, or zircon in the evening can also help.

INTESTINAL DISORDERS (Including indigestion, irritable bowel syndrome and cancer.) Carry or wear chevron amethyst, **citrine**, dravite, fulgurite, green fluorite, halite, obsidian, peridot, or tiger's eye. Hold crystals to areas of discomfort.

IODINE DEFICIENCY Carry or wear garnet.

IRON DEFICIENCY Carry or wear **bloodstone**, bronzite, chlorite, or vanadinite. **Blue opal** is helpful in cases where too much iron is present.

JAUNDICE Carry or wear aquamarine, carnelian, **citrine**, emerald, or jasper.

JAW, FROZEN Hold fluorite to affected area for 20–30 minutes. Repeat as required.

JET LAG Carry hematite + turquoise on air journeys.

JOINTS, CALCIFICATION (Including arthritis.) Hold flint to each affected joint for 20–30 minutes daily.

JOINTS, DEGENERATIVE DISEASE Hold cleavelandite to affected joints for 20–30 minutes every day.

JOINTS, FLEXIBILITY Carry, wear and hold to relevant joints: **azurite/malachite**, petalite, or septarian.

KIDNEY, DYSFUNCTION Carry or wear amber, aquamarine, bloodstone, bornite, calcite, **carnelian**, chrysoberyl, citrine, emerald, jade, jasper, opal, picture jasper, prehnite, rhodochrosite, rose quartz, tsilasite, uvarovite, or white calcite.

KIDNEY STONES Hold flint to the kidney area for 30 minutes daily.

KNEE, INJURY OR STIFFNESS Hold **apache tear** or smoky quartz to the knee.

LACTOSE INTOLERANCE Carry or wear spessartine.

LARYNGITIS Hold **blue calcite**, hawk's eye, or stilbite to the throat for 20–30 minutes as required.

LEGS, GENERAL ACHES AND PAINS Hold **goshenite** or smoky quartz to the affected area. Also place in bottom of bed at night. **Chrysocolla** can be effective for cramp in the legs.

LETHARGY Carry or wear carnelian, **copper**, coral, or peridot. Hold when feeling particularly tired. Alternatively, hold two **orange calcite** stones, one in each hand, to restore energy balance.

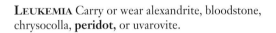

Pour fresh water over your chosen crystal to make an elixir (see page 23). Check first that your crystal is safe to use in an elixir (see the Crystal Finder, pages 32–103).

LEUKEMIA Carry or wear alexandrite, bloodstone, chrysocolla, **peridot,** or uvarovite.

LIGAMENT INJURY Hold **dumortierite,** magnesite, or stilbite to the injured ligament.

LIGHT SENSITIVITY Carry or wear **rhodonite. Selenite** can help with skin symptoms.

LIVER, DYSFUNCTION Carry or wear almandine, amethyst, aquamarine, azurite/malachite, bloodstone, carnelian, chevron amethyst, chrysoberyl, citrine, danburite, **emerald,** flint, golden ray calcite, heliodor, imperial topaz, iolite, jasper, peridot, tsilasite, yellow fluorite, or white calcite. Hold to liver area to relieve discomfort.

LIVER SPOTS Carry or wear **chlorite** or selenite and hold to each spot for 5–10 minutes daily.

LONGEVITY Carry or wear **jade,** petrified wood, ruby, or selenite.

LUMBAGO Tape fluorite to lower back at the center of the discomfort.

LUNG CAPACITY, REDUCED Carry or wear a chrysocolla pendant to encourage increased lung capacity.

LUNG DISEASES Wear a pendant or carry adamite, aventurine, carnelian, chalcopyrite, chevron amethyst, **chrysocolla,** dioptase, elbaite, flint, garnet, hiddenite, indicolite, kunzite, larvakite, morganite, opal, peridot, pink opal, pyrite, rhodolite, rubellite, topaz, turquoise, vanadinite, uvarovite, watermelon tourmaline, or zoisite.

LYMPH, EXCESSIVE FLUID Carry or wear aquamarine to enhance the performance of the lymphatic system.

LYMPH NODES AND VESSELS, INFLAMED Carry or wear agate, hessonite, jade, sodalite, **tourmaline,** or white calcite.

MAGNESIUM DEFICIENCY Carry or wear chlorite, garnet, or **serpentine.**

MALABSORPTION OF FOOD/NUTRIENTS, LACK OF This is usually a result of other conditions such as Crohn's disease. Carry or wear **citrine,** idocrase, reversed watermelon tourmaline, sphalerite, turquoise, turritella agate, or yellow opal. These crystals promote the speed of uptake of nutrients, which will increase the speed of healing.

MALARIA Carry or wear **iolite** or staurolite.

MASTITIS Hold amethyst to discomfort in breast.

ME (MYALGIC ENCEPHALOMYELITIS) Carry or wear **rhodochrosite + rhodonite + topaz** all the time. Work with other specific crystals to alleviate symptoms. Carnelian, gray banded agate, petalite, and quartz can also be helpful.

MELANOMA Carry or wear chlorite or **gold.** Hold crystal to affected area for 30 minutes daily. Place septarian in your immediate vicinity.

MÉNIÈRE'S DISEASE Hold dioptase to the ear for 30 minutes or as long as it is bearable. Repeat as often as possible, at least daily.

MENINGITIS Place an amethyst cluster next to the bed. See specific symptoms to help relieve discomfort.

MENOPAUSE Carry or wear carnelian, garnet, lingham, moonstone, or **ruby** all the time. Hold any of these when symptoms are active.

MENORRHAGIA (ABNORMALLY HEAVY MENSTRUAL FLOW) Carry, wear, or hold goethite until bleeding subsides.

MENSTRUAL CYCLE To regulate the menstrual cycle, carry or wear jade, **moonstone**, rose quartz, **ruby,** or selenite all the time for three complete cycles.

METABOLISM To boost metabolism carry, wear or place around you sodalite, pietersite or **copper**. To decrease metabolism, try blue opal, **blue quartz**, chrysocolla, diamond, nephrite, Picasso marble, or pyrolusite.

MIGRAINE Hold the darkest purple amethyst as close as you can to the site of pain until you feel better. Carry the same crystal with you all the time to reduce the frequency of attacks.

MINERAL DEFICIENCIES Carry or wear **gold** or jasper.

MOLES Apply an elixir of marcasite to your skin.

MONONUCLEOSIS Place muscovite in your immediate vicinity and next to your bed at night.

MOUTH DISORDERS Place a washed citrine tumble-polished stone in your mouth for 10–15 minutes several times a day, or carry **covellite** and hold in your hand while mentally focusing on your mouth.

MOUTH ULCERS Hold citrine or **dioptase** to the white spots.

MS (MULTIPLE SCLEROSIS) Carry or wear aventurine, gold, hematite, **jade**, jasper, quartz crystal, or titanium quartz. Hold to areas of discomfort. See also specific symptoms.

MUCOUS MEMBRANE DISORDERS (For example, cystic fibrosis). Carry or wear blue fluorite. Hold close to affected area as required.

MUSCLE RUPTURE Hold or tape **rainforest rhyolite** to source of discomfort. Alternatively, hold **lapis lazuli crystal** or malachite to damaged muscle for 20–30 minutes. Repeat often during the day.

MUSCLE, SORE Carry or wear **aventurine**, chrysocolla, fuchsite, jade, kyanite, tiger iron, turquoise, or zircon. Hold to injuries or discomfort. A septarian elixir can also help.

MUSCLE SPASM Hold **apache tear** to affected muscle.

Place **zebra rock** at the foot of your bed. For persistent conditions carry or wear apache tear.

MUSCLE SPRAIN/STRAIN Hold Brazilian agate, dalmatian stone, **solomite**, or **sphene** to affected muscle.

MUSCLE STIFFNESS Hold **danburite**, petalite, or stibnite to affected muscle. For persistent conditions carry or wear **petalite**.

MUSCLE TONE Drink rhyolite elixir each morning.

MYOPIA Carry or wear aventurine and place on eyelid for 20–30 minutes daily.

NAIL DISEASES AND DISORDERS Hold blue lace agate, **dolomite,** or sandstone to nails for 20–30 minutes daily.

NAUSEA Hold **citrine**, dioptase, green fluorite, obsidian, sapphire, or tiger's eye until the feeling abates. (Also consider the emotional causes of nausea.)

NEAR-SIGHTEDNESS Carry or wear peridot and place on eyelids for 20–30 minutes daily.

NERVE DAMAGE Carry or wear **alexandrite** and hold to affected area for at least 30 minutes daily. To speed up nerve impulses after nerve damage, carry or wear zincite and hold to affected areas.

NERVES, ACTIVATING/STIMULATING Hold rutilated quartz to affected areas. For general stimulation hold two crystals – one in each hand.

NERVES, TRAPPED OR PINCHED Carry or wear jasper or **lepidolite** and hold to affected areas.

NERVOUS SYSTEM DISORDERS Carry or wear **amazonite**, aquamarine, aventurine, azurite, beryl, dioptase, epidote, **gold**, pink banded agate, **sphalerite**, tourmalinated quartz, or variscite. For conditions that affect the autonomic/sympathetic nervous system, such as dysautonomia, carry or wear amethyst, and either place under the middle of your back or keep a cluster on your bedside table at night.

NEURALGIA Carry or wear **aquamarine + aventurine + rutilated quartz** or carnelian. Hold to painful areas until pain eases.

NOCTURNAL VISION Carry or wear fire agate or **tiger's eye** at night. Place on eyelids for 5–10 minutes just before it gets dark.

NOSEBLEED Hold **bloodstone** or magnetite to nose until bleeding stops.

NUTRITIONAL BALANCE Carry or wear dioptase all the time. Place next to your bed at night.

OBESITY Carry or wear cassiterite, **chalcedony + quartz crystal**, cinnabar, or citrine all the time. Place a quartz crystal cluster next to your bed at night. Sit quietly and focus your thoughts on your crystals for at least 30 minutes daily.

OLD AGE (degeneration) Carry **sapphire** and hold it at times when you feel "old". Carry or wear sodalite. See also **YOUTHFUL APPEARANCE**.

OSTEOPOROSIS Carry or wear cavansite, **smithsonite**, or zebra rock. Hold to painful areas for 30 minutes each.

OVARIAN DISORDERS See **REPRODUCTIVE SYSTEM DISORDERS**

PAIN (GENERAL) Hold a **quartz crystal** point a little above the site of pain and move it slowly in a clockwise direction. Continue until pain eases. Boji stones, celestite, chevron amethyst, chlorite, hemimorphite, howlite, and rose quartz can also ease pain – hold or tape them to the affected area. An elixir of dioptase can act as an analgesic.

PANCREAS DAMAGE Hold charoite to the area of discomfort.

PANCREAS, DISEASES OF Carry or wear agate, alexandrite, almandine, beryl, blue lace agate,

PREVENTING ILLNESS

Some crystals are renowned for keeping you healthy and protecting against illness. Carry, wear, and keep these around you: angel aura quartz, boulder opal, hemimorphite, iolite, jasper, jet, lapis lazuli crystal, nephrite, orbicular jasper, rainbow fluorite, **red jasper**, ruby, titanium quartz, or wavellite. You can also drink a glass of topaz elixir each morning to keep you healthy.

calcite, carnelian, cassiterite, chevron amethyst, crysoberyl, **chrysocolla**, heliodor, herderite, malachite, peridot, rubellite, or zoisite. Also hold to the area of discomfort.

PARALYSIS Carry or wear gold, or tape it to the affected areas.

PARASITES Place serpentine in rooms and carry a piece with you.

PARKINSON'S DISEASE Carry or wear **alexandrite**, cerussite, epidote, opal, or rutilated quartz all the time.

PERIOD PAIN Carry or wear **chrysocolla**, jade, kunzite, or moonstone. Hold to area of discomfort until pain subsides. Carry or wear crystals all the time for three months to help prevent pain.

PERISTALSIS, SLOW To treat symptoms such as bloating, indigestion, nausea, and wind, carry or wear **hawk's eye** or turritella agate.

PHLEBITIS Carry or wear galena and hold to area of discomfort.

PHYSICAL WORK Wear coral. Place larger piece of coral in your work area.

PILES See **HEMORRHOIDS**

PINEAL GLAND The pineal gland is implicated in a number of disorders including cancer, sexual dysfunction, hypertension, epilepsy, and Paget's disease. Lie down and place amethyst, opal, pietersite, **sugilite,** or zircon on your brow or third eye for 30 minutes daily.

PITUITARY GLAND, DYSFUNCTION Hold or place amethyst, aventurine, malachite, moonstone, opal, pietersite, sapphire, **sugilite,** or zircon on the back of your neck near the top.

PMS/PMT (**PREMENSTRUAL SYNDROME/ PREMENSTRUAL TENSION**) Carry or wear **chrysocolla**, jade, kunzite, magnesite, moonstone, or ruby all the time for three months. Hold these when you notice symptoms.

PNEUMONIA Carry or wear gold or place it next to your bed.

POISONS Carry or wear copper, **diamond**, hemimorphite, peridot, stilbite, sunstone, or zircon for protection and treatment.

POST-OPERATIVE HEALING Place almandine, amber, boji stone, coral, fuchsite, jadeite, leopard skin rhyolite, scapolite, or **turquoise** next to the bed. Play with any of these in your hands and hold to areas of discomfort.

POST-OPERATIVE PAIN Drink dioptase elixir as required.

POSTURE Carry or wear amethyst.

PREGNANCY Carry or wear **chrysocolla**, moonstone, or unakite to relieve uncomfortable symptoms. Carry or wear chrysocolla as it helps the healthy development of the unborn child. Hold ruby to the belly for the health of the embryo.

PRESSURE SORES Hold **aventurine + fuchsite** or **selenite** to the affected area for 30 minutes twice daily until symptoms clear.

PROLAPSE OF THE WOMB Carry or wear jade on or around the belly.

PROSTATE, INFLAMMATION OF (PROSTATITIS) Carry or wear lingham, **variscite**, or zincite.

PSORIASIS Hold **gypsum**, **selenite**, or turquoise to the worst affected area for 30 minutes daily. Put aragonite in your bath water to create a giant topical elixir. Also look at possible emotional causes.

PUPIL AND IRIS DISORDERS To improve control of pupil contraction and dilation (which affects light sensitivity), place clear fluorite on your eyelid. For long-sightedness, short-sightedness, squint, lazy eye, and double vision, place clear fluorite or **scapolite** on your eyelid for 5–10 minutes.

PURIFICATION, OF BODY Wear amber.

RADIATION Protect yourself by carrying or wearing herkimer diamond. Wear or carry pietersite, **schorl**, or turquoise. Pyrite can help to treat radiation sickness.

RASHES Hold rhyolite to skin for 5–10 minutes and repeat often as necessary.

Holding turquoise to the throat area can help the vocal chords.

RECTAL PROBLEMS Carry or wear citrine or **tiger's eye** to help disorders including rectal prolapse or inflammation.

RED BLOOD CELLS To treat problems such as anemia, carry or wear bronzite, **erythrite**, garnet, or sphene.

REFLEXES/REACTION TIME To improve reflexes, carry or wear aventurine or **reversed watermelon tourmaline.**

REPRODUCTIVE SYSTEM DISORDERS (For example, cancer, ovarian cysts, abnormal vaginal bleeding, and sexually transmitted infections). Place **chalcanthite** next to your bed. Carry or wear crocoite, **falcon's eye,** or rubellite. Also hold these crystals to areas of discomfort.

REPRODUCTIVE SYSTEM, FEMALE, DISORDERS Hold, carry, or wear jade – can help with most conditions including endometriosis and ovarian cancer.

RESPIRATORY PROBLEMS (For example, shortness of breath, hyperventilation, uneven breathing, or sleep apnea.) Carry or wear **turquoise** or gold.

RESTLESS LEG SYNDROME Place chrysocolla or **jadeite** at the bottom of your bed. If symptoms persist, carry or wear crystals all the time.

RHEUMATISM Hold **chrysocolla + copper**, garnet, gold, lodestone, malachite, melanite, sunstone, or turquoise to affected joints. Carrying or wearing these crystals may also help.

RHINITIS Hold blue fluorite to your nose for 2–5 minutes and repeat every hour until symptoms stop.

SALT IMBALANCE Carry or wear bornite or place it next to your bed.

SCAR TISSUE Hold amber or **citrine** on the scar for 30 minutes daily to speed healing.

SCIATICA Carry or wear zircon. Hold to areas of pain.

SCLEROSIS OF THE LIVER Carry or wear charoite all the time.

SEASICKNESS Carry or wear aquamarine to prevent seasickness. Hold this crystal to ease symptoms.

SELENIUM DEFICIENCY Carry or wear galena, or place it next to your bed.

SENSE OF SMELL, LACK OF Carry or wear coral, jasper, or **idocrase** to enhance your sense of smell.

SEX DRIVE, EXCESS Selenite calms an over-active sex drive.

SEX DRIVE, LACK OF Agate, **black calcite**, garnet, jet, merlinite, rose quartz, rutile, and **smoky quartz** can revive sexual interest.

SHINGLES Place **amethyst** cluster next to bed and hold **selenite** to skin blisters. Work with a **quartz crystal** point directly on painful areas.

SICKNESS See **NAUSEA**

SIDE EFFECTS, OF MEDICATION Carry, wear, or hold melanite.

SINUS PROBLEMS Carry or wear **jade** or hold to your nose/face as required. **Snowflake obsidian** connects the meridian from the sinuses to the stomach and can be very helpful if stomach symptoms are also present.

SINUSITIS Hold jade to your nose/face as required.

SKIN, AFTER SUN Place stilbite next to your bed after a day in the sun.

SKIN DISORDERS and irritations including dry, itchy skin, eczema, psoriasis, dermatitis, shingles, pressure sores, and erythema (redness of the skin). Carry or wear amethyst, aventurine, dolomite, erythrite, **fuchsite**, gold, gypsum, kunzite, kyanite, magnetite, picture jasper, quartz crystal, **selenite**, tanzanite, wavellite, or zincite. Hold to required area and place crystals next to bed at night. Apply to your skin an elixir of elbaite, **green moss agate**, moonstone, pink opal, or topaz, or drink an elixir of crazy lace agate, epidote, jade, or snowflake obsidian.

SKIN, DRY Place zebra rock next to your bed.

SKIN ELASTICITY Carry, wear, or hold **selenite** or variscite to your skin or apply gypsum elixir to skin.

SKIN GROWTHS Hold **blue lace agate** to site. Wash in marcasite elixir or drink a flint elixir for superficial growths.

SKIN, HARD Hold aragonite to affected area.

SKIN, SENSITIVE Drink **Brazilianite** elixir daily and hold **selenite** to affected areas.

SKIN, STRESS-RELATED DISORDERS Drink **aragonite** or turquoise elixir.

SNORING Place pyrite under your pillow.

SORES Hold emerald to the affected area.

SPEECH Carry or wear blue fluorite, **blue lace agate**, crazy lace agate, celestite, carnelian, citrine, or silver, and hold when you need to say important things.

SPEECH IMPEDIMENTS Carry or wear silver.

SPEEDS/INCREASES THE EFFECTS OF OTHER CRYSTALS Carry, wear, hold with other crystals, place on other crystals, or place on the body: diamond or **drusy chrysocolla**.

SPINAL CANAL, DAMAGE TO Carry or wear coral.

SPINAL FLUID, IMBALANCE Lie down and place garnet on or under your back.

SPLEEN, ENLARGED This can be due to many diseases; it is vital to treat the underlying cause. Carry, wear, or hold alexandrite, aquamarine, bloodstone, blue quartz, calcite, carnelian, chrysoprase, fluorite, heliodor, **hematite**, herderite, jade, jasper, malachite, peridot, pink opal, rhodochrosite, rose quartz, tsilasite, or zoisite to the area of the spleen.

SPONDYLITIS Lie on stomach and place **dumortierite + selenite** on the affected area. In addition, place one piece of **hematite** at the bottom of your spine and another piece at the top.

SPOTS Hold dravite or **smithsonite** to each spot for 10–15 minutes daily.

STAMINA, LACK OF Carry, wear, or place around you: **anhydrite**, dalmatian stone, dumortierite, okenite, or metamorphosis quartz. Zebra rock is particularly helpful for athletes. Drink a rhyolite elixir.

STAMMER Carry or wear **blue lace agate**, celestite, silver, or smoky quartz.

STIES Hold gold to sty.

STOMACH DISORDERS Many disorders can show similar initial symptoms. The following crystals can help the different underlying causes of the symptoms. Hold or place on stomach: amethyst, **citrine**, dioptase, green fluorite, jasper, mookaite, sapphire, smithsonite, stibnite, tiger's eye, tsilasite, or turritella agate. For chronic conditions carry or wear any of these all the time. **Snowflake obsidian** can unblock the meridian between the nose and stomach, so try this if you also have nasal symptoms. Jet is helpful for stomach ache.

STRESS-RELATED PHYSICAL CONDITIONS (Including asthma, allergies, skin conditions, ulcerative colitis, and heart disease.) Carry or wear azurite/malachite, cleavelandite, **kunzite**, lepidolite, or nephrite. Handle and play with these crystals often.

STROKE Place cleavelandite or **melanite** near bed.

SWELLINGS Hold anhydrite, **aquamarine**, bornite, malachite, moonstone, or sulfur to the affected area.

SWOLLEN GLANDS Hold aquamarine + sapphire to the site of swelling for 10–30 minutes. Repeat several times a day as required.

SUNBURN Hold **falcon's eye + peridot**, rose quartz, or sphene to the affected area. Apply hematite elixir to your skin or drink Brazilianite elixir.

SUNSTROKE Hold or place brazilianite next to your bed.

TASTE, LOSS OF Place stilbite or **topaz** on your tongue for 5 minutes daily until taste returns.

CRYSTAL CLEANSERS

Cleansing or detoxing is a vital part of the healing process. As toxins, pollutants, and other substances are released from your body, your natural relaxation response kicks in and tension flows away. Your skin improves and many physical conditions, ailments, illnesses, and diseases – even long-term, chronic ones – seem to ease or disappear completely. There is no one magic crystal that does this for everyone, but there are many crystals listed here that could be your personal magic crystal: abalone shell, amber, amethyst, apache tear, bloodstone, celestite, chalcopyrite, chevron amethyst, barite, chlorite, citrine, copper, covellite, danburite, diamond, garnet, gold, green opal, herkimer diamond, hessonite, Iceland spa, iolite, malachite, opal, orbicular jasper, peridot, petalite, Picasso marble, pink banded agate, rose quartz, ruby, silver, snowflake obsidian, spirit quartz, stilbite, topaz, tourmaline, turquoise, ulexite, uvarovite, white calcite, yellow fluorite, and zeolite. You can also try elixirs of charoite and nebula stone.

Try one or two of them – whichever you are drawn to. Keep them with you all the time. Place them under your pillow or on your nightstand. Hold them and play with them and see what happens over two weeks. Persist with these and add others from this list. Some, just like friends, will be needed for a little while, whereas other crystals will stay around you forever.

Tear ducts Place blue fluorite on your face (under your eyes by your nose).

Teeth/toothache Carry or wear amethyst, aquamarine, azurite/malachite, cavansite, coral, dolomite, emerald, **fluorite**, howlite, magnesite, malachite, sphene, or zebra rock. Hold to skin near painful teeth. Use a septarian elixir as a mouthwash.

Temperature balance Carry, hold, or wear **green opal**, magnesite or pietersite.

Temperature, high Carry, hold or wear aquamarine.

Temperature, low Carry, hold, or wear gold.

Tendon disorders (For example, tendonitis.) Hold or tape **dumortierite**, lepidolite or magnesite to the affected area.

Tension (physical) Carry or wear **abalone shell**, ametrine, cerussite, herkimer diamond, mahogany obsidian, or rose quartz. Hold at night for 10 minutes before going to sleep and then place next to your bed.

Testicular cancer Carry opal + peridot in trouser pocket and place in your bed at night.

Thalamus Carry or wear coral.

Thirst Carry a carnelian pebble to reduce thirst. Traditionally, this is sucked when needed.

Throat, infection Place **blue calcite**, erythrite, or rhodonite on the throat for 30 minutes daily until symptoms abate.

Throat, sore Hold **green fluorite** or sunstone to the throat for a few minutes until the soreness eases.

Amethyst promotes a calm ambience.

Throat disorders For example, vocal chord nodules and polyps. Carry or wear adamite, amber, angelite, anhydrite, apatite, aquamarine, blue fluorite, **blue lace agate**, bornite, covellite, fulgurite, goethite, hawk's eye, **indicolite**, **kyanite**, lapis lazuli, or **turquoise**. Hold to throat as required. For long-term problems place crystal on throat for 30 minutes daily.

Thymus, over- or underactive Work with angelite, chevron amethyst, citrine, indicolite, lapis lazuli, or **verdelite**.

Thyroid gland disorders Overactive, underactive and thyroiditis: Carry or wear aquamarine, carnelian, chrysocolla, citrine, epidote, halite, **indicolite**, lapis lazuli, or mookaite, and hold to the throat when needed. For underactive thyroid, carry or wear **garnet**.

Tinnitus Move a quartz crystal point slowly in a clockwise direction pointing into the ear until symptoms improve. Repeat if symptoms reappear.

Tiredness Carry or wear blue opal or **copper**.

Tiring effects of computer screens Place **fluorite** (natural crystals work best) or pietersite between you and the screen (or on desk near screen).

Tissue regeneration (For example, after injury or surgery.) Carry or wear amber, apatite, apophyllite pyramid, boji stones, carnelian, **citrine**, garnet, gold, malachite, pyrite, topaz, turquoise, or rutilated quartz. Hold any of these to the affected area. Tiger iron increases steroid production which aids tissue repair.

Tonsillitis Place shattuckite on the throat for 30 minutes daily until symptoms disappear.

Tooth enamel, damaged Carry or wear idocrase.

Trace elements Carry or wear turritella agate to aid absorption.

Transplants Carry or wear ametrine to help avoid tissue rejection.

Trapped nerve Hold blue lace agate to the pain.

Travel sickness Carry or wear aquamarine, **hematite + turquoise,** or moonstone. In case of severe symptoms, hold until symptoms cease.

TUBERCULOSIS Carry or wear chrysocolla, gold, morganite, or **topaz**. Also place next to your bed.

TUMORS Carry or wear malachite, **peridot**, petalite, or selenite. Hold to areas of discomfort.

ULCERS Hold azurite/malachite, **dioptase**, fluorite, hemimorphite, or sunstone close to the ulcerated area. In severe cases carry or wear these crystals.

UROGENITAL SYSTEM DISORDERS (For example, urine infections, incontinence, prostate disease, and cancer.) Carry or wear aventurine, **dolomite**, or kyanite. Hold to or place on areas of discomfort.

VARICOSE VEINS Hold or tape agate, **dioptase**, pyrite, rose quartz, or rainforest rhyolite to area.

VASCULAR DISEASE Carry or wear gold.

VD (VENEREAL DISEASE) Carry or wear hemimorphite.

VEINS, DAMAGED, THINNING/THICKENING Carry or wear galena, rhyolite, rutile, **scapolite**, smithsonite, or snowflake obsidian; or hold or tape to affected area.

VERTIGO Carry or wear **lapis lazuli**, rose quartz, or zircon. **Blue fluorite** helps vertigo and dizziness – hold against the ear.

VIRAL INFECTION Hold or place **amethyst**, emerald, jade, or nephrite to or on the affected area.

VISION Place citrine on the eyelids. See **EYESIGHT**

VITALITY Carry or wear any of the following: anyolite, beryl, bloodstone, blue quartz, **carnelian**, cassiterite, cinnabar, common opal, crazy lace agate, dioptase, emerald, **garnet**, gold, lapis lazuli, mahogany obsidian, orange calcite, rubellite, rutilated quartz, schorl, smithsonite, smoky quartz, spessartine, sunstone, tiger iron, topaz, yellow opal, or zincite. Cerussite is helpful after illness.

VITAMIN DEFICIENCIES Carry or wear **gold** or zebra rock. For vitamin A deficiency carry or wear aragonite, chlorite, garnet, grossularite, or silver. For vitamin B deficiency carry or wear pyromorphite, rhyolite, or tiger iron. For vitamin C deficiency carry or wear apache tear or chrysoprase. For vitamin D deficiency carry or wear apache tear, aragonite, or garnet. For vitamin E deficiency carry or wear chlorite, garnet, or silver.

VOICE Carry or wear blue calcite, carnelian, or **kyanite**. Hold to or place on the throat.

VOMITING Hold **citrine** or hemimorphite until symptoms stop.

WARTS Hold, tap, or gently rub **labradorite** on warts or apply an elixir of **marcasite** to the affected area.

WATER RETENTION Carry or wear anhydrite, **aquamarine**, chalcanthite, halite, mookaite, moonstone, sandstone, or titanium quartz. Hold to areas of swelling.

WEIGHT GAIN Carry or wear coral, danburite, fluorite, goethite, peridot, rutilated quartz, **sphalerite**, **turquoise,** or unakite.

WEIGHT LOSS Carry or wear cassiterite, chalcedony, hemimorphite, iolite, mookaite, Picasso marble, quartz crystal, verdelite, or **yellow fluorite**. Hold for 30 minutes each evening and focus on losing weight. Drink a large glass of **chlorite** elixir each morning.

WHIPLASH Carry or wear coral or **turquoise**. Place aqua aura on neck for 30 minutes daily until better.

WIND PAINS Hold, carry or wear agate, chlorite, **citrine**, jasper, thulite, turquoise, turritella agate, obsidian, tiger's eye, or variscite to the discomfort.

WOUNDS Hold almandine, **bloodstone**, flint, sandstone, topaz, or turquoise to the wound. Wash wound with pyrolusite or rutile elixir.

WRINKLES Carry or wear aragonite, **rose quartz,** or selenite. Drink lepidolite elixir.

YOUTHFUL APPEARANCE Add rough **rose quartz** to your bath, and carry or wear kunzite, moonstone, okenite, rhodochrosite, rose quartz, rutilated quartz, sapphire, selenite, or sodalite.

ZINC DEFICIENCY Carry or wear galena.

Remedies for emotional ailments

Try the crystal(s) in **bold** in the following entries first, and then the others. Where a + sign joins two or more crystals, they should be worked with in combination. The more you work with the same crystal(s) for the same condition, the quicker and more effective it will be.

With all emotional conditions, carry or wear the crystals all the time. Hold them and play with them, too. Place larger crystals in any room in which you spend a lot of time (for example, your bedroom, living room, or workplace). Follow any specific instructions given.

Be aware that the symptoms in this section can be linked to either current or past stresses or trauma. Current trauma can be relieved with gold, **manganoan calcite,** and tree agate. Trauma and issues that are linked with the past can be helped with alexandrite, anhydrite, **blue chalcedony**, bowenite, **dalmatian stone**, **eudialyte**, larvakite, muscovite, **obsidian**, rose quartz, scapolite, spirit quartz, and unakite.

Childhood experiences can affect you consciously or subconsciously; **blue chalcedony**, diamond, eudialyte, rose quartz, and tourmalinated quartz help to bring these experiences to the fore. They allow you to recognize and release bad experiences, capitalize on the good ones, and understand the spiritual lessons the past may have brought. Amazonite, **larimar**, larvakite, and moonstone can soothe you during this process.

Emotional conditions are often so upsetting that, before you begin to process them, you need simply to calm down. Useful crystals in this case are ajoite, amazonite, amber, amethyst, aquamarine, aventurine, blue fluorite, blue lace agate, bloodstone, **calcite** (all varieties), dalmatian stone, fuchsite, kunzite, kyanite, lepidolite, malachite, manganoan calcite, merlinite, mookaite, moonstone, Picasso marble, prehnite, rhodolite, rhodonite, rose quartz, rutilated quartz, serpentine, smithsonite, sodalite, strawberry quartz, thulite, tiger's eye, tourmaline, tree agate, uvarovite, variscite, and zircon. **Ametrine** promotes serenity and **smoky quartz** can have an almost tranquillizing effect.

ABUSE, PHYSICAL, SEXUAL, OR VERBAL Hold **amber** or **selenite** for 30 minutes each day. Continue daily even if you feel upset as hidden emotions begin to flow. It may take many months for wounds to heal. Verdelite and manganoan calcite can also help. **Blue chalcedony** is helpful in cases of child abuse.

ACALULIA (DIFFICULTY WITH MATHEMATICAL CALCULATIONS) Snowflake obsidian can aid your ability to do simple mathematics.

ADDICTIVE BEHAVIOR Work with amethyst and **chalcedony.**

AGGRESSION Bloodstone, cinnabar, larimar, and orange calcite will soften aggressive feelings, **amethyst** and **pink opal** can stem violent tendencies, while **bloodstone** (heliotrope variety) or emerald can lessen bad temper.

AGING Diamond, **rhodochrosite**, rutilated quartz, sapphire and sodalite can help the mental and emotional symptoms associated with old age. Also try placing several pieces of rough rose quartz into your normal bath – relax, light candles, and listen to gentle music or a spoken meditation. Ajoite, alexandrite, almandine, okenite, and **wulfenite** can all promote a youthful attitude to life.

AIMLESSNESS Thulite can help you find direction in life.

ANGER AND RESENTMENT Ajoite, **amethyst**, angelite, aragonite, blue quartz, chlorite, citrine, diamond, gold, hemimorphite, howlite, idocrase, magnetite, **melanite**, muscovite, peridot, smoky quartz, and sugilite alleviate feelings that range from slight annoyance to total rage. For quick release of anger hold carnelian, howlite, quartz, or **snowflake obsidian** when needed.

ANIMOSITY Melanite can reduce the feeling of hatred toward others.

ANTI-SOCIAL BEHAVIOR Work with galena or **pearl**.

ANXIETY Aquamarine, **aventurine**, azurite/malachite, blue quartz, calcite (all varieties), cerussite, chrysoprase, citrine, green moss agate, labradorite, Picasso marble, rhodonite, and **schorl** can calm anxiety.

APATHY Carnelian revives your interest in everyday life and activities.

APPREHENSION Excitement and apprehension may be difficult to differentiate. **Blue quartz** helps you recognize and enjoy excitement. **Larvakite** releases apprehension so you can move on.

ARGUMENTATIVE TENDENCIES Work with flint and **grossularite**.

BEREAVEMENT See **GRIEF**

BOREDOM Work with quartz, citrine, garnet, and **spessartine**.

BROKEN HEART Work with **chrysocolla** and chrysoprase. **Elbaite** bathes the heart in loving energy.

BURDENS Work with gold, lodestone, and **scapolite**. **Amethyst** helps you cope with negative feelings about your responsibilities.

CENTERING, LACK OF Aventurine, bloodstone, and **titanium quartz** help center you.

COMPULSIVE BEHAVIOR Work with chalcedony, kunzite, and **lepidolite**.

CONCENTRATION, POOR Work with amazonite, aventurine, fulgurite, petrified wood, pyrite, and **snow quartz**. Kyanite, **lapis lazuli,** and okenite help you concentrate for longer.

CONFIDENCE, LACK OF Bronzite, **crazy lace agate**, dumortierite, jade, moonstone, pyromorphite, and sugilite boost confidence. **Muscovite** and okenite clear self-doubt.

CONFUSION Apatite clears disorder in your mind. Carnelian, **lodestone**, rhodonite, and sodalite can help when you find yourself perplexed with everything in life.

CONTROL, LACK OF Falcon's eye, fire agate, **moonstone**, pearl, and septarian help you control your emotions when necessary. However, emotional control is a short-term fix and can cause emotional blockages. Ultimately, emotions must be released rather than stored and controlled.

Rose quartz can help dispel envy.

COURAGE, LACK OF Aquamarine, bloodstone, carnelian, crazy lace agate, diamond, garnet, hematite, hessonite, idocrase, jade, nebula stone, rhodochrosite, sardonyx, sugilite, **tiger's eye,** and turquoise can give you the strength to be brave.

CRISIS Work with **rose quartz**. **Okenite** gives you the equivalent of a cuddle.

CYCLES AND REPEATED PATTERNS Charoite, **chrysoberyl**, moonstone, silver, topaz, and tsilasite help to break negative cycles in work, relationships and other aspects of life. **Chrysoprase** helps you to recognize patterns and the ways in which they may hinder you.

CYNICISM Work with quartz, **chrysoberyl**, grossularite, Iceland spa, and merlinite.

DARK SIDE Wulfenite helps you to see, face, and deal with your dark side.

DEATH AND DYING PROCESS Almandine, anhydrite, black banded agate, chiastolite, cocoite, lepidolite, and **morganite** promote acceptance of death and can ease the passing of spirit from the physical body to the next world.

DEPRESSION Aqua aura, black opal, bowenite, coral, garnet, gold, idocrase, jet, kunzite, lapis lazuli, lepidolite, malachite, mookaite, peridot, quartz, rutilated quartz, sapphire, smoky quartz, staurolite, tiger's eye, **tourmalinated quartz,** and zircon all help. **Danburite** is helpful for post-operative depression.

DESPAIR Celestite, **rutilated quartz**, smoky quartz, sugilite, and variscite help when you feel you don't have any answers and that you have nothing left to give

DESTRUCTIVE BEHAVIOR Work with elbaite.

DISTRESS Crocoite or ruby can ease concern and suffering.

DREAD Work with smoky quartz + tourmaline.

ECCENTRICITY Sugilite helps you accept and live with your eccentricities.

EGOISM/SELFISHNESS Azurite/malachite, gold, **hemimorphite**, howlite, marcasite, peridot, and **tree agate** help to level your opinion of yourself. See also **SELF-IMPORTANCE**

EMOTION, EXCESSIVE Adamite, calcite, coral, crocoite, moonstone, **rose quartz**, serpentine, unakite, and watermelon tourmaline help balance the emotions. **Melanite** calms excessive emotion.

EMOTIONAL BLOCKAGES Amber, **diamond**, and peridot help release blocked feelings. Abalone shell, ametrine, **apache tear**, blue quartz, Brazilianite, **eudialyte**, green moss agate, **larvakite**, moonstone, **muscovite**, phantom quartz, and **spirit quartz** allow you to be brave and let your feelings out.

EMOTIONAL DISTANCE Flint promotes closeness between people, helping a relationship to grow.

EMOTIONAL ENERGY, LACK OF Agate, amethyst, **bornite**, jet, moonstone, and spinel boost your emotional energy. **Mahogany obsidian** gives you strength in times of need.

EMOTIONAL IMBALANCE Alexandrite, amethyst, apache tears, aquamarine, beryl, blue lace agate, blue quartz, calcite, copper, crazy lace agate, garnet, jade, malachite, moonstone, rose quartz, sapphire, silver, and turquoise bring stability to your emotions. Blue lace agate, **dioptase**, garnet, schorl, and variscite can help you hold your emotions together.

EMOTIONAL POISONS/TOXINS Citrine cleanses the hurt you feel as a result of other people's words and actions.

EMOTIONAL STAMINA, LACK OF Okenite keeps you going even if you feel emotionally battered.

EMOTIONAL WOUNDS Cobaltoan calcite or **rose quartz** help to heal wounds. **Aventurine**, lime green tourmaline, and petrified wood can soothe the emotions. **Ruby** heals deep pain or anguish. **Fuchsite** lifts you and aids recovery after you have been hurt.

EMPATHY, LACK OF Angel aura quartz, azurite and **idocrase** promote compassion, sympathy, and understanding.

ENDINGS Apatite and moonstone soothe the emotions that are tied up with endings (for example, the end of a relationship or a job). Small endings can be difficult because they can catch you unawares; big endings can be difficult because you may end up preparing yourself so much that you block the release of your emotions.

ENERGY, EXCESS Brazilianite and **strawberry quartz** channel away energy you are not using. This relaxes you and leads to a peaceful night's sleep.

ENERGY VAMPIRES These are people who drain energy from you, so that you feel tired or exhausted after seeing them. Aventurine helps stop others leeching your energy.

EXHAUSTION, NERVOUS Tourmalinated quartz releases nervous energy.

EXPRESSIVENESS, LACK OF Azurite, howlite, muscovite, and sodalite help you to express your feelings.

FEAR Work with ajoite, aquamarine, aventurine, calcite, carnelian, chlorite, chrysoprase, crazy lace agate, fire agate, **herkimer diamond**, idocrase, **jet**, magnetite, mookaite, moonstone, nebula stone, picture jasper/picture stone, pietersite, prehnite, rose quartz, sodalite, sunstone, tiger's eye, topaz, tourmalinated quartz, and **tourmaline**. **Bowenite** relieves acrophobia, and **spirit quartz** is helpful if you're frightened of succeeding.

FEEBLENESS Kyanite enhances perseverance and dispels frailty and weakness.

FEELING DOWN Jasper helps to lift your mood. Amazonite, calcite, carnelian, chrysocolla, chrysoprase, copper, lepidolite, peridot and **quartz crystal** are all "feel good" crystals. They make you feel better and improve the quality of your life. Keep them around you even when you're feeling fine – life will start to feel even better.

FEELINGS, NOT BEING AWARE OF Verdelite helps you know how you feel about something without the interference/judgement of the outside world.

FEMININITY, LACK OF Work with abalone shell, black calcite, chrysocolla, kunzite, **moonstone**, **pearl**, **pink banded agate**, and rose quartz.

FORGIVENESS, LACK OF Apache tear, chrysoberyl, **eudialyte**, **rose quartz**, and sugilite promote a forgiving attitude.

FRUSTRATION Work with rose quartz.

GRIEF Amethyst, angelite, **apache tear**, aqua aura, bornite, bowenite, dolomite, magnetite, onyx, picture jasper/picture stone, rose quartz, **smoky quartz,** and spirit quartz can ease grief and the pain of bereavement.

GROUNDING, LACK OF Bixbyite, black agate, black calcite, black obsidian, black opal, blue quartz, boji stone, cassiterite, cerussite, galena, green opal, **hematite**, jade, jasper, larvakite, lodestone, magnetite, mookaite, obsidian, petrified wood, Picasso marble, pietersite, red calcite, smoky quartz, stilbite, and tiger's eye can all be helpful for grounding. **Agate** and calcite help to put your feelings into perspective.

AMETHYST FOR AFTERSHOCK

Amethyst promotes calm after a stressful encounter, such as a confrontation, and working with this crystal can also help you deal with the effect of little stresses that build up throughout the course of a day, month, and even over a number of years.

When you begin to feel stressed, it's important to take yourself away from the situation that has caused the stress as quickly as possible. Take hold of two amethyst crystals, one in each hand. Wait a minute or two until you notice that you are feeling calm and your breathing returns to normal. If you work with your crystals every time you feel even slightly stressed, you will quickly find that fewer things stress you and you relax more easily after each stressful event. Aquamarine, celestite, lapis lazuli, and smoky quartz can also promote a relaxed state of mind and body.

GUILT Work with chrysocolla, larimar, and **rose quartz**.

GUT FEELINGS, ACCESSING Magnetite, **tiger's eye,** and yellow opal help you to recognize and trust your gut instincts. This helps you avoid stress.

HEART, CLOSED Sometimes your heart closes to avoid pain. Eudialyte opens the heart to love.

HOMESICKNESS Amethyst, cerussite, and meteorite relieve the longing for home and reminds you that home is where you are at this moment.

HOPELESSNESS Boulder opal inspires optimism when all else fails.

HOSTILITY Chlorite and sugilite help. **Orange calcite** eases belligerence and promotes gentleness.

ILLUSION Work with rainforest rhyolite.

IMMATURITY Kunzite is helpful for anyone behaving significantly and consistently younger than their age.

IMPATIENCE Aragonite, dumortierite, **emerald,** orbicular jasper, marcasite, septarian, sheen obsidian, and spirit quartz promote patience.

INADEQUACY Rose quartz and sodalite soothe feelings of failure.

INCOHERENCE Meteorite assists mental and emotional understanding.

INCONSISTENCY Contrary behavior can be as confusing to you as to others. Rhodonite can help bring consistency to your actions and emotions.

INDECISION Work with citrine, aventurine, Brazillianite, wavellite, fluorite, onyx, titanium quartz, Iceland spa, cerrusite, **topaz**, stibnite, bronzite, muscovite, amethyst, mookaite, and ruby.

INFERIORITY COMPLEX Chrysoprase, **gold,** hessonite, and sphalerite are all helpful in overcoming a sense of inferiority.

INHIBITION Barite, **opal,** and tiger's eye reduce shyness and stop you holding back.

INNER-STRENGTH, LACK OF Adamite and black agate can help you connect to your inner power.

INSECURITY Agate, angelite, aventurine, boulder opal, **labradorite,** larvakite, lodestone, and muscovite promote a feeling of security and protect your emotions.

INSENSITIVITY AND OVER-SENSITIVITY Moonstone, rhodonite, and selenite promote sensitivity. **Sodalite** thickens a thin skin. **Amethyst** helps to bring balance. Work with either moonstone or sodalite together with amethyst.

INTROVERSION Blue quartz, cerussite, and tiger's eye help you to be more extrovert.

IRRATIONALITY Azurite/malachite, grossularite, kyanite, and sulfur enhance rationality and reasoning.

IRRITABILITY Work with chalcedony and **pearl**.

JEALOUSY/ENVY Work with carnelian, peridot, **rose quartz** and **melanite**.

LAZINESS/LETHARGY Carnelian, coral, **peridot,** and zoisite can give you a boost and get you moving.

LONELINESS When you are alone and feeling isolated jasper, mookaite, snowflake obsidian, **spirit quartz,** and **uvarovite** help you cope.

LOSS Aqua aura and **morganite** ease loss. **Unakite** helps soothe the loss of an ideal or dream.

LOVE, UNREQUITED Fuchsite helps to heal the heart when your feelings are not returned.

LOVELESSNESS Abalone shell, almandine, angel aura quartz, barite, bowenite, celestite, **diamond**, elbaite, kunzite, magnesite, manganoan calcite, morganite, pink opal, rainbow obsidian, **rose quartz**, strawberry quartz, turquoise, and watermelon tourmaline all promote and help you find love.

MALEVOLENCE Jade reduces wicked tendencies and promotes benevolence.

MANIPULATION See **MIND GAMES**

MANIC DEPRESSION Kunzite, **lepidolite**, and malachite are helpful for treating extreme swings of emotion.

MASCULINITY, LACK OF Work with **black obsidian**, lingham, **obsidian**, **smoky quartz**, and variscite.

MENTAL APATHY Work with ruby, **rutilated quartz**, and smoky quartz when you feel you can't get your brain working. **Golden ray calcite**, imperial topaz, and tsilasite also get your mind working again.

MENTAL BALANCE, HEALTH AND HEALING Alexandrite, amethyst, aquamarine, **celestite**, chrysoprase, dioptase, garnet, gold, heliodor, idocrase, moldavite, peridot, petrified wood, phenacite, rhodonite, ruby, **rutilated quartz**, rutile, **silver**, sodalite, **sugilite**, sulfur, tiger's eye, and **tourmaline** all help to maintain mental wellbeing.

MENTAL BLOCKS For those times when you feel blocked and nothing comes to mind, try ametrine, rutilated quartz, snow quartz, and **tourmaline** to let your thoughts flow freely.

MENTAL BREAKDOWN If it feels like the world is falling apart, chalcedony, **rhodochrosite**, **rutilated quartz,** and **tourmaline** can gently bring you back to the world.

MENTAL UNREST Rhodonite, Iceland spa, **white calcite**, and **sodalite** help to calm, still, and settle the mind. To ease a troubled mind try amazonite or **tourmaline**. For severe mental trauma work with silver and **yellow fluorite**. Drinking a **pink opal** elixir can be calming and comforting for all types of mental rest, whether mild or severe.

MIND, FULL UP Achroite, boulder opal, covellite, pink opal, **snow quartz**, turquoise, and ulexite clear the mind, creating space to think. **Chrysoprase**, **diamond**, ulexite, and white calcite help you see through the fog.

MIND GAMES Iceland spa helps you see through deception and avoid confusion.

MIND, LACK OF CLARITY Anyolite, **celestite**, spessartine, **tsilasite,** and **yellow fluorite** promote clear thoughts, allowing ideas to surface and opening your mind to new and potentially amazing levels of inspiration.

MIND, UNFOCUSED Hold **fluorite**, labradorite, pearl, phenacite, **quartz crystal**, or zincite and focus your thoughts on the crystal. After 10–20 minutes, any mental confusion will have gone, enabling you to focus on anything you want to.

MOOD SWINGS Halite and sandstone can calm the emotional pendulum.

NARCISSISM Work with okenite.

NEGATIVITY This is a state of mind, but it is highly susceptible to the environment around you. When you feel negative you draw negativity to you, and when the atmosphere around you is full of negative energy you are easily brought down. **Amber**, apatite, aqua aura, aquamarine, **cassiterite**, coral, dalmatian stone, **diamond**, flint, gold, hematite, hessonite, jade, merlinite, pyrite, pyrolusite, quartz, rainforest rhyolite, rutilated quartz, **schorl**, silver, **smoky quartz**, snow quartz, **tiger's eye**, **topaz**, **tourmaline**, **turquoise**, **verdelite**, and zoisite protect you from negativity. They help you release negative energy held in your aura and they enhance your sense of wellbeing. **Chrysocolla** is useful for transmuting negative emotions into positive feelings.

NEGATIVITY, SUPPRESSED Apache tear helps release any negativity you are holding onto, whether you are aware of it or not.

Carry turquoise to ease travel stress.

NERVES, EXAM Amazonite calms the nerves; **aventurine** is good for physical tension; and **snow quartz** clears the mind allowing you to both study and stay focused on the exam. These three crystals work fantastically together.

NERVOUS BREAKDOWN See **MENTAL BREAKDOWN**

NERVOUSNESS AND TENSION Abalone shell, **amazonite**, amethyst, golden ray calcite, chevron amethyst, chrysocolla, gold, green moss agate, lepidolite, muscovite, and **watermelon tourmaline** calm the nerves and reduce tension.

NIGHTMARES Place **celestite**, flint, gold, manganoan calcite, or ruby under your pillow.

OBSESSION Fixation on anything or anyone is destructive and leads to sacrifices in your personal everyday needs. This damages your wellbeing and, eventually, your health. Chalcedony helps obsessions.

OBSESSIVE BEHAVIOR Work with **spirit quartz**. To treat OCD (obsessive-compulsive disorder) work with amethyst, **chalcedony**, and red calcite.

OBSESSIVE PASSION Work with blue topaz and **stibnite**. **Chrysoprase** helps you to see and break behavior patterns.

OBSTINACY See **STUBBORNESS**

OPPRESSION Work with dioptase.

OVER-ATTACHMENT Magnetite reduces over-attachment and neediness leading to clearer energy around you. Once you let go of people, issues, and things, you find the ones you really need are still there; the others are gone, creating a space for new encounters to come into your life. **Prehnite** and rainforest

Tiger's eye helps you get in touch with your gut instincts.

rhyolite help you release old feelings and move on in life; for example, at the end of a relationship or job, or when moving house. **Anhydrite** promotes your ability to accept situations, which facilitates further release. **Lodestone** and **iolite** reduce dependence and the need to hold on.

OVER-ENTHUSIASM Calcite calms eagerness without diminishing interest. Copper and **fluorite** lessen over-excitement.

PAIN, COPING EMOTIONALLY Bixbyite can help you cope emotionally with physical pain and suffering.

PANIC ATTACKS As soon as you feel an attack coming on hold a **green calcite** or red calcite crystal. Focus on the crystal and imagine the fear starting to disperse and flowing into the crystal.

PARANOIA Work with chalcedony.

PASSION, EXCESS Amethyst calms passion. See also **OBSESSIVE PASSION**

PASSION, LACK OF Herderite, magnesite, **moonstone**, **opal**, **rhodochrosite**, and ruby boost passion and allow it to flow.

PERSONALITY BLOCKS We can stop our true character from showing, either deliberately or unconsciously. **Diamond** removes blocks – both self-imposed or from your upbringing – allowing your personality to shine. **Amethyst** can soothe your temperament leading to a calmer disposition.

PESSIMISM Moonstone and **muscovite** give you a more optimistic outlook.

PHOBIAS Aquamarine, **chrysocolla**, and rose quartz help to dispel irrational fears.

POST-TRAUMATIC STRESS Work with garnet, yellow fluorite, gold, tree agate, **bowenite**, green fluorite, manganoan calcite, rhodochrosite, coral, and silver.

PREJUDICE Ajoite, **ametrine**, **aquamarine**, cassiterite, septarian, and sugilite help to reduce prejudice and promote tolerance. **Chrysoprase** or cleavelandite help you to accept others. Judgmental attitudes are softened by aquamarine, **chrysoprase** and **metamorphosis quartz**. General bigotry and

CRYSTALS TO DE-STRESS

Sometimes you may feel so overwhelmed by what you have to do within a day that you feel stressed – physically and emotionally drained. You crave sleep, but sleep may be elusive – and you don't feel at all rested when you get up the next morning. When you get into this state, try holding any of the crystals listed below. Sit quietly holding the chosen crystal in your hand and begin to let yourself relax by becoming more aware of your breathing. Picture it raining outside. Gradually allow time to slow down. Feel yourself becoming more calm and centered inside. Imagine the rain stopping and the sun coming out. Imagine a beautiful rainbow appearing in the sky.

You can practice this effective visualization whenever you feel the need, for a few minutes each day or longer, if you can make more time for yourself. Choose from any of the following crystals: amazonite, aragonite, bloodstone, calcite, celestite, chalcedony, chrysocolla, chrysoprase, fluorite, green moss agate, hematite, herkimer diamond, howlite, labradorite, peridot, petrified wood, Picasso marble, quartz, rainbow obsidian, rhodochrosite, rose quartz, staurolite, sunstone, or topaz. The crystal should be a comfortable size in your hand – not too small, nor too large, so it fits naturally in your palm and feels good to touch. Keep your crystals close by, either in your pocket or bag, so that you can hold them and begin to feel more calm whenever the need arises.

narrow mindedness can be diminished with **tiger's eye** or sapphire.

PMT/PMS (PREMENSTRUAL TENSION/SYNDROME) Changes in hormones during the menstrual cycle can cause emotional as well as physical symptoms. You may feel tired and ratty, and have unpredictable mood swings. **Chrysocolla**, jade, kunzite, moonstone, and ruby can soothe all the symptoms of PMT/PMS.

PROCRASTINATION Rainforest rhyolite allows you to recognize and overcome the obstacles that prevent you from doing something.

REJECTION Cassiterite helps you cope.

RESTLESS MIND Chrysoberyl, moonstone, morganite, petalite, snowflake obsidian, strawberry quartz, **tourmaline**, turquoise, and **verdelite** calm your brain and promote peace of mind.

RESTLESSNESS Copper and **manganoan calcite** calm restlessness. Ametrine, angel aura quartz, and **manganoan calcite** promote peacefulness.

SADNESS Aqua aura, **carnelian**, **dolomite**, **meteorite**, and quartz crystal help to relieve sorrow and lift melancholy. Blue quartz, bornite, dalmatian stone, **quartz crystal**, rainbow obsidian, and sapphire all promote happiness.

SCHIZOPHRENIA Work with amazonite + amber + aventurine + chrysoprase + jade + rhodonite + tourmaline.

SELF-ACCEPTANCE, LACK OF Chrysoprase helps you see and accept yourself as you are. It blows away the clouds covering your heart and lets you look into your soul.

SELF-CONTROL, LACK OF Onyx enhances control. **Dalmatian stone** and moonstone promote composure.

SELF-ESTEEM, LOW Alexandrite, amethyst, carnelian, citrine, crazy lace agate, kunzite, lepidolite, mookaite, nebula stone, **opal**, rhodonite, sodalite, spirit quartz, and zircon boost your sense of worth. **Cinnabar** can help give you back your dignity.

SELF-HATE Ajoite and **okenite** help to remove negative feelings. **Eudialyte** and diamond promote self-love.

SELF-IMPORTANCE Common opal helps you find a balance between thinking too much and too little of yourself. Conceit is diminished with azurite/malachite and **thulite**. **Jade** enhances modesty.

SELF-NEGLECT Sometimes you spend so much time and effort looking after others that you forget about yourself. Chrysoberyl helps you to think of yourself as well.

SENILE DEMENTIA Alexandrite and chalcedony can help slow deterioration. They are most helpful at the beginning of illness.

SEXUAL FRUSTRATION Chrysoprase and rose quartz.

SEXUAL QUALITIES, IMBALANCE All of us have a feminine and a masculine side. Sometimes life events cause them to become out of balance. To restore this balance work with amber, ametrine, apatite, aventurine, **black banded agate**, calcite, celestite, chalcedony, chrysoprase, citrine, common opal, dalmatian stone, dioptase, hematite, iolite, jasper, jet, kyanite, lapis lazuli, lodestone, merlinite, **moonstone**, nephrite, onyx, petalite, rhodochrosite, rhodonite, rhyolite, sphalerite, tektite, tiger's eye, tourmaline, turquoise, ulexite, and unakite.

SHALLOWNESS Zebra rock brings substance and depth to your character.

SHOCK Tree agate is very soothing. It calms you physically, emotionally, and spiritually and helps to restore your equilibrium.

SHOPAHOLICISM Smoky quartz helps you to recognize your basic underlying needs and the changes you need to make to fulfil them; it helps you move forward to a more fulfilled, happier life.

SHORT-TEMPER See **IRRITABILITY**

SHYNESS Barite helps you overcome timidity and promotes a sense of boldness.

SPONTANEITY, LACK OF Work with apache tear, **blue quartz**, and herkimer diamond.

STRESS See **ANXIETY** and **WORRY**

STRESS, 21ST CENTURY This means running around, trying to do too much and trying to be in too many places at once. Beryl, **imperial topaz**, rhodochrosite, rhodonite, and topaz can get to the source of your troubles. In cases of complete burnout, **fire opal** can re-energize you.

STUBBORNNESS Dumortierite helps you become more flexible in your outlook.

SUBCONSCIOUS BLOCKAGES Obsidian aids the release of energy unknowingly trapped in your body or mind, usually related to a past event or issue. Apache tear, **bornite**, bowenite, galena, and unakite help you see the blocks you put in your own way and allow you to move forwards in life.

SUBCONSCIOUS MIND, TROUBLED By definition, we have no idea what is in our subconscious. Yet unknown thoughts can affect us negatively. **Boulder opal** and Picasso marble help bring thoughts into consciousness.

SUFFERING Ruby eases the pain.

SUPERIORITY COMPLEX Chrysoprase and **turritella agate** help you be more humble. **Apatite** reduces

EMOTIONAL GROUNDING

When you are grounded, energy moves freely through your body and any excess flows away from you into the earth. This means that your subtle energies remain in balance and, on an emotional level, you feel focused, present, and in control. The short-term effect of not being grounded is a feeling of uneasiness which many people describe as nervousness or restlessness. Things that wouldn't normally bother you have a negative effect and you may get easily irritated or upset.

The longer-term effects of being ungrounded are an imbalance in your subtle energy that can lead to burn-out – when you feel you can simply no longer cope – or health problems. However, if you cultivate an awareness of when you are losing your ground or center, you can take steps to reverse this.

Try the following exercise: Sit on the floor with your legs crossed or in any other comfortable position. Hold a piece of hematite in your hands. Contemplate the stone. Touch it and feel its textures and contours. Look at it and then close your eyes and picture it in your mind's eye. Do this several times. Bring your awareness to the point of contact between your body and the ground. Let any weight and tension you are carrying sink down through your body and flow out of you into the earth. It can help to imagine that you are a plant – the upper part of your body is light, free, and flexible like the stem and the leaves. The lower part is weighted and connected with the ground like strong, sturdy roots. To finish, open your eyes and very slowly, stand up.

Rainforest rhyolite stops procrastination, helping you to make decisions.

aloofness. Arrogance can be diminished with azurite/malachite, **blue topaz,** or chrysoprase.

SUSPICIOUS MIND Turquoise reduces obsessive suspicion and allows you to be more trusting. **Lepidolite** and melanite may also be helpful.

TACTLESSNESS Chrysocolla encourages tact.

TANTRUMS Muscovite and sandstone help to reduce the frequency and ferocity of tantrums.

TRAGEDY Nebula stone helps you cope in heart-rending circumstances.

TRAUMA Garnet, **rhodochrosite,** and rose quartz help to soothe emotional shocks. Green fluorite is beneficial in milder cases.

TRAVEL WORRIES Moonstone and **turquoise** calm concerns associated with journeys.

TURMOIL Jade promotes feelings of peace and tranquillity within you.

UNCARED FOR FEELINGS Angel aura quartz, chalcedony, and **pink banded agate** promote the feeling of being nurtured.

UNCARING FEELINGS Moonstone promotes a caring attitude toward others.

UNFOCUSED Carnelian, **fluorite,** and **quartz crystal** are useful when you need to concentrate. They all help you hold your attention for longer and keep your mind focused.

VANITY Azurite/malachite, covellite, and thulite help you see through your own image and take yourself less seriously.

VICTIM MENTALITY Schorl, tourmaline, and turritella agate give you a feeling of protection allowing you to be less defensive and stop blaming everyone else for your troubles.

VULGARITY Howlite tempers hilarity with restraint.

WILFULNESS Sulfur reduces headstrong, obstinate behavior.

WILL TO LIVE, LACK OF Azeztulite, black agate, and **ruby** all promote the desire to live and can have an impact on critical conditions.

WORRY Work with celestite, muscovite, **Picasso marble,** and tiger's eye.

WORRY WHAT OTHERS THINK Coral and **tourmaline** give you a feeling of protection and inner strength that frees you from concern about how others see or judge you.

Crystals for spiritual enhancement

We all follow our own unique spiritual path through life. When we stay on this path, energy flows, life moves forward, and we feel healthy and happy. When we stray from our path, energy stagnates, life moves sideways or back, and we feel stressed and tense. If you are unsure of what your path or purpose in life is, barite, **cobaltoan calcite**, idocrase, prehnite, stibnite, sugilite, thulite, and titanium quartz can bring direction. **Pink opal** is great to work with at the start of your spiritual journey – it promotes an awakening within you. If you feel delayed on your spiritual path, **sheen obsidian** is good to work with. **Charoite**, clear fluorite, lingham, and obsidian can help you bring your spiritual experiences into your physical world and daily life. Ametrine will bring understanding. Boulder opal, **cobaltoan calcite**, rainbow obsidian, and tree agate can help you to see the beauty in everything. Try the crystal(s) highlighted in **bold** first, and then the others.

AKASHIC RECORDS, ACCESSING Angel aura quartz, merlinite, nebula stone, pietersite, sapphire, and **record keeper ruby** help you gain access to this mystical knowledge.

ANGELS AND GUARDIAN SPIRITS, ACCESSING **Angel aura quartz**, **angelite**, **celestite**, **goethite**, and **petalite** enhance your connection to the angelic realms.

AURA, CLEARING The aura holds a record of everything that has happened in your life. Sometimes the "dark bits" of energy that represent illness and stress group together in a mass. The energy that naturally flows through the aura can make these dark elements dissipate but, when this fails to happen, there may eventually be dis-ease in the area of the body close to where the dark elements are massed. Carry or wear amazonite, angel aura quartz, **aqua aura**, coral, **gold** (gold jewelry is a mixed metal and does not work efficiently in this case; work with a gold nugget or gold

in quartz), ametrine, boji stone, boulder opal, citrine, clear fluorite, dravite, garnet, iolite, jasper, petalite, pyrolusite, rainbow obsidian, rutile, tourmaline, and zircon.

AURA PROTECTION AGAINST UNWANTED ENERGIES Carry or wear agate or **diamond**. A diamond set in jewelry is fine, but don't use an engagement ring as this is specifically for the purposes of love, loyalty, and devotion.

AURA STABILIZATION (Feeling "wobbly".) Carry or wear coral or **labradorite** and keep a piece next to your bed.

AURA, STRENGTHENING To boost your energy field, carry or wear agate or **zircon**.

CENTERING, SPIRITUAL This means reaching a point of inner stillness from which you can observe the world moving around you. Aquamarine, bixbyite, **boji stones (in a pair)**, galena, green opal, and kunzite help to bring you to this point. These crystals are beneficial for people who feel they are always moving and can't stop. The crystals don't prevent you from doing things; they simply allow you to relax while you go about your daily life – you find a certain comfort inside yourself. Continue working with these crystals to find a deeper meaning to life. See also **MEDITATION**

CEREMONY Beryl, cerussite, chalcedony, gypsum, **kyanite**, **morganite,** or staurolite promote a sense of ceremony and ritual. Carry them or place them within the sacred circle or ceremonial area. Blue lace agate, **herkimer diamond,** and kyanite amplify the attunement process. **Smoky quartz** protects you from any unwanted energies that may be present.

CHAKRAS All crystals work on your chakra/energy system. (See chapter 3 for the specific chakras that are associated with individual crystals.) Apatite and **boji stone pairs** balance all your energy centers. **Green fluorite** is good for detox; **aquamarine** removes blocks; **kyanite** aligns the major chakras; and labradorite promotes the flow of energy between your aura and chakras.

CONNECTION TO ANCESTORS Abalone shell, bowenite, **obsidian,** and onyx link you to your roots.

CONNECTION TO GOD There are many names for a higher being or energy: God, Goddess, Buddha, Jesus, Mohamed, The Tao, Universal Life Force Energy, All That Is, and many others. Amethyst, bixbyite, blue quartz, chalcopyrite, fire agate, **gold**, onyx, petalite, **snow quartz**, tibetan quartz, turquoise, and **ruby** enhance your connection to a higher being or plan. Your own personal understanding of spirituality is boosted by chrysoberyl, **emerald**, hiddenite, and tiger's eye.

CONNECTION TO SPIRIT Work with **ajoite**, **amethyst**, angelite, **anyolite**, apophyllite, aventurine, barite, **blue fluorite**, blue quartz, carnelian, fire agate, goethite, kyanite, morganite, petalite, sapphire, sugilite, sunstone, **tanzanite,** and wulfenite to sense spirit guides and the essence of all living things.

DEVOTION Work with chiastolite, dalmatian stone, garnet, kyanite, **ruby,** and **sapphire.**

PSYCHIC PROTECTION

Our psychic energies are challenged on a daily basis. Intentional attacks or uncaring words, thoughtless remarks, gestures, and general negativity from other people around you can all bring you down.

Energy depletion can also be more subtle. Those who work as therapists and carers can pick up empathic pains and even symptoms from their clients throughout the day. Yet you don't need to be a carer to have a similar experience – in the same way, people who pour out all of their troubles to you may leave you feeling low. Neighbors who drop round for a few minutes stay for an hour and unknowingly, they've taken your energy, leaving you feeling tired and drained. However, certain crystals can stop this happening to you.

Try any of the following: angel aura quartz, aqua aura, black calcite, black obsidian, brazilian agate, cassiterite, dalmatian stone, diamond, dravite, fire agate, jade, kunzite, magnetite, nephrite, obsidian, pyrite, rutile, schalenblende, schorl, sphalerite, spirit quartz, staurolite, and tourmaline. Drinking an angelite elixir daily can also be effective. Amber and jet can protect you from violence; red jasper in combination with jet can protect you from witchcraft. Heliodor will look after things while you are away; such as your family, car, and home – a perfect crystal to leave at home while you're staying elsewhere. Idocrase makes you aware of danger so you can avoid it; and sardonyx keeps you safe from crime. Stibnite guards you from "evil spirits", and smoky quartz sends any bad intention back to its source, so whoever sent it will get it right back, speeding up the laws of karma!

DISTANT HEALING Work with **apophyllite**, **ruby**, silver, tiger's eye, and topaz.

DREAMS, NIGHT TIME **Celestite**, green opal, jade, kyanite, **lapis lazuli**, larvakite, moldavite, mookaite, prehnite, red jasper, ruby, and spirit quartz help you to both have and remember your dreams. Dream interpretation is facilitated by kyanite, larvakite, malachite, and **smoky quartz**.

HIGHER-SELF AND INNER-SELF Almandine, apatite, aquamarine, **bi- and tri-colored tourmaline**, blue quartz, emerald, fluorite, garnet, **imperial topaz**, lingham, malachite, moonstone, muscovite, **phantom quartz**, **prasiolite**, rainbow obsidian, rutilated quartz, **spirit quartz**, thulite, topaz, snowflake obsidian, sodalite, spirit quartz, tourmaline, ulexite, uvarovite, **watermelon tourmaline,** and wulfenite increase your awareness and insight and help you connect to that deep inner-most bit of you that you know is the true you. Some people call this the soul, spirit, chi, life-force or essence. **Silver** clears a path through you so you can look right into your heart; and **obsidian** acts as a "mirror of the soul".

KARMA Angel aura quartz and **okenite** help you to understand karmic issues. Bornite speeds the process of karma so you don't take it into your next lifetime.

LOVE Amethyst, **crazy lace agate**, elbaite, pink banded agate, rhodonite, **rose quartz**, and sugilite promote a feeling of unconditional, spiritual or universal love.

PAST LIVES, ACCESSING Alexandrite, cerussite, dioptase, eudialyte, **petrified wood**, spirit quartz, and **unakite** facilitate access to past life experiences. **Apatite**, boulder opal and golden ray calcite aid recall.

PURITY Boulder opal, **peridot**, **diamond**, snowflake obsidian, **snow quartz**, and **pearl** enhance spiritual purity.

SOULMATES, FINDING Bowenite, **uvarovite**, wulfenite, and zircon can help you find and link with your spiritual partner. This may or may not involve a physical relationship.

SPIRITUAL BALANCE Amethyst, **quartz crystal**, ruby, and **sapphire** bring stability to your personal spiritual path.

SPIRITUAL DETOX Diamond, lingham, **phenacite**, star ruby crystal, and ulexite clear unwanted energies from your spirit.

SPIRITUAL DEVELOPMENT Amazonite, aquamarine, celestite, moonstone, snowflake obsidian, and **tourmaline** boost your spiritual growth.

TOTEM ANIMALS Angelite, leopard skin rhyolite, petalite, and **stibnite** help you to identify and connect with your spirit animals.

VIRTUE This is one of the traditional spiritual values in many cultures and is promoted by sapphire.

WISDOM Beryl, cerussite, **jade**, coral, gold, lapis lazuli, moonstone, morganite, obsidian, ruby, sapphire, snow quartz, turquoise, and zircon promote insight, knowledge, understanding and good judgment.

Crystals for lifestyle enhancement

ABUNDANCE, MONEY, AND WEALTH Adamite, amethyst, **cinnabar**, **citrine**, diamond, dioptase, garnet, gold, green moss agate, lepidolite, phenacite, ruby, spirit quartz, sunstone, tektite, tiger's eye, topaz, tourmaline, and verdelite can all be helpful in the acquisition of both wealth and material items. **Citrine**, known as the "money stone", attracts riches – keep a crystal in your pocket or coin purse. Amethyst, **cinnabar**, and ruby help you focus on money matters, and iolite and stibnite can aid financial management. If you are addicted to the material world, try working with **larimar** to let it float away.

ACCIDENT, PREVENTION If you are accident prone, **jade**, pyrite, and reversed watermelon tourmaline protect you.

ACTIVITY, PROMOTING Carry or wear beryl or place it in your workspace.

AMBITION, DREAMS, GOALS, AND IDEALS **Sapphire** helps you find balance in your ambitions. It brings realism to the over-ambitious and adds drive and direction where needed. (The key word is "needed" not "wanted".) Achroite, amber, bowenite, chalcanthite, cleavelandite, covellite, dalmatian stone, dioptase, howlite, jade, jasper, mahogany obsidian, scapolite, and vanadinite are all helpful in your quest for a more fulfiled lifestyle. Amethyst, cinnabar, **ruby**, topaz, and verdelite promote success.

ANIMALS, HEALING AND COMMUNICATION **Rainforest rhyolite** helps to heal animals, and **boji stone** aids communication with them.

APPRECIATION Nebula stone allows you realize the value of everything around you. It promotes gratitude towards people, your environment, and the universe.

BEAUTY Spinel brings out your looks and personality.

BEST FEATURES Chrysoberyl and zircon bring out your best characteristics in any circumstances. Azeztulite helps you make the best of every situation.

BRAIN, LEFT/RIGHT BALANCE This is the place where intellect meets intuition and science and magic converge. **Bornite**, **diamond**, **labradorite**, and **tourmaline** bring a state of equilibrium between the left and right brain.

CHALLENGES, NEW Tourmaline helps you face new challenges giving you feelings of strength and courage. It will open your mind to the positive benefits of the test and help you see the way forward.

CHANGE **Metamorphosis quartz** lets you see the changes you need to make to your lifestyle and facilitates transformation. **Eudialyte** and iolite ease the process of change and soothe your emotions, gently bathing your heart center in healing energy. Amethyst, ametrine, apache tear, black banded agate, bowenite, cerussite, chiastolite, diamond, dioptase, garnet, lepidolite, moonstone, Picasso marble, pyrolusite, rhyolite, ruby, scapolite, sheen obsidian, titanium quartz, and turritella agate also promote change. **Crocoite** helps to ease the really big shifts that take place in life.

CHILDREN, COPING WITH Mookaite helps you cope with the demands of children.

COMMUNICATION AND EXPRESSION These crystals assist both spoken and written communication: angelite, apatite, **aqua aura**, aquamarine, barite, blue calcite, blue chalcedony, **blue lace agate**, blue opal, **blue topaz**, **chalcanthite**, fulgurite, heliodor, howlite, **indicolite**, kyanite, lapis lazuli, purple fluorite, reversed watermelon tourmaline, shattuckite, sodalite, **tanzanite**, topaz, and **turquoise**. **Mookaite** improves communication skills. **Erythrite** aids conversation. **Blue quartz** helps you express what's in your mind. **Barite** assists with the explanation of ideas, and **achroite** promotes expression of profound thoughts. Your physical expression through body language can be improved with **smoky quartz** whilst **flint** helps you to understand others. Public speaking is made easier with amethyst, **septarian**, and turquoise.

CREATIVITY All of these inspire creativity: ajoite, alexandrite, amazonite, ametrine, aventurine, azurite, black obsidian, bloodstone, blue opal, bixbyite, cavansite, **celestite**, cerussite, chiastolite, chrysocolla, **citrine**, crocoite, diamond, elbaite, golden ray calcite, goshenite, hemimorphite, imperial topaz, **indicolite**, mookaite, moonstone, blue opal, picasso marble, pink banded agate, rhyolite, rose quartz, rubellite, ruby, schorl, sodalite, sphalerite, stilbite, tiger iron, topaz, tourmaline, tsilasite, **yellow fluorite**, ulexite, verdelite, and zincite.

DECISION-MAKING Choices are made easier with amber, **amethyst**, aventurine, brazilianite, bronzite, cerussite, chalcanthite, **citrine**, fluorite, iceland spa, mookaite, onyx, rainforest rhyolite, ruby, sandstone, and stibnite. **Muscovite** can help with the really major decisions in life. Aragonite, black banded agate, blue opal, **chevron amethyst**, chiastolite, green opal, **jade**, muscovite, **phantom quartz**, pink banded agate, rhyolite, scapolite, and tourmalinated quartz help you find answers to life's problems.

DESIRE Brazilianite, kunzite, and magnetite bring desires to the surface. This allows you to see if you really want them or not. Sapphire helps control.

DIVORCE Crocoite and melanite can ease this difficult time and help you remain rational and composed through the process. Grossularite and **smithsonite** can help you solve any disputes.

ENVIRONMENTAL ISSUES Septarian increases your awareness of environmental issues. **Chrysocolla**, larimar, and turritella agate promote Earth healing. **Dravite** is a great crystal to work with if you want to save the planet. **Lodestone** can help if you suffer from the effects of geopathic stress. **Dravite**, prasiolite, rainbow obsidian, and schorl enhance your connection to nature.

FLOW Amethyst, apache tear, **aquamarine**, charoite, garnet, goshenite, gypsum, kunzite, merlinite, mookaite, okenite, rhodochrosite, smoky quartz, and spirit quartz make everything flow better in life. Things that were stuck become fluid – life moves forwards. If you need it, black opal and **topaz** can give you momentum.

FRIENDSHIP Barite, bowenite, **rose quartz**, and **turquoise** help you make new friends. **Blue opal** and **blue quartz** connect you to people and are also good for networking.

FUN AND HUMOR Goethite, pyromorphite, and **watermelon tourmaline** help you see the funny side of situations and life in general.

HOUSE If you are selling your home, place a **citrine** crystal in each room to speed the sale. The experience of moving is made easier with **bowenite**, and if you are emigrating, **meteorite** can ease the transition.

INSPIRATION Achroite, **ametrine**, carnelian, fire agate, labradorite, nebula stone, opal, orange calcite, **prehnite**, rhodolite, sulfur, and **tourmaline** free your mind, allowing brainwaves and flashes of genius to appear. **Diamond**, dolomite, idocrase, and tsilasite inspire invention. **Beryl** allows you to take the initiative. Individuality and uniqueness are supported by **azurite/malachite**, and topaz. Bixbyite, coral, **diamond**, opal, rose quartz and ulexite allow your imagination to flow freely. Adamite and **scapolite** promote lateral thinking.

LEADERSHIP Aventurine, herderite, onyx, **pyrite**, and smithsonite promote leadership. **Lapis lazuli** aids organizational skills and fluorite can help bring order out of chaos.

LEARNING/STUDY Aquamarine, calcite, carnelian, citrine, dalmatian stone, galena, gold, hiddenite, howlite, lepidolite, obsidian, **purple fluorite**, ruby, and **snow quartz** all aid the pursuit of knowledge.

LIVING IN THE PRESENT The present is the only moment that exists – the past has gone and the future isn't here yet, so don't let yourself dwell on them. **Dioptase**, **iolite**, and **unakite** help you live in the moment. **Merlinite** helps you seize the moment.

LUCK Everyone needs luck from time to time. Alexandrite, gypsum, hemimorphite, moonstone, onyx, sardonyx, staurolite, **tiger's eye**, and **turquoise** can tip the scales in your favor.

NEGOTIATION SKILLS Amethyst and **tourmaline** help you reach agreement.

NEW BEGINNINGS The start of anything new such as projects, relationships, and jobs, is assisted by black banded agate, citrine, **diamond**, elbaite, herkimer diamond, **hessonite**, moonstone, pyromorphite, ruby, schalenblende, smithsonite, tiger's eye, and **tourmaline**.

NOISY NEIGHBORS Place pyrite on each of your window ledges and your life will almost instantly be quieter.

RELATIONSHIPS Hematite, imperial topaz, magnetite, and **stibnite** help you attract new partners. **Boulder opal** increases your sexual attractiveness. Brazilianite, cerussite, citrine, cleavelandite, dalmatian stone, fluorite, goshenite, iolite, lapis lazuli, pyrolusite, **rose quartz**, sandstone, zincite and zircon promote healthy, loving relationships. **Chrysocolla** revitalizes, jadeite and **morganite** repair, and **charoite** helps to release old relationships. **Agate** and stibnite promote faithfulness, and **sardonyx** promotes marriage or partnership. **Rose quartz** and turquoise bring out romance. Sexuality may be liberated with **copper**, crocoite, or falcon's eye.

REVITALIZING Danburite helps you re-enter the world after you've been away for any reason; such as illness, recuperation, rehabilitation, or prison.

SMOKING CESSATION Kunzite and staurolite help you quit the habit.

SOCIAL SKILLS Danburite and sardonyx help you interact with others.

SPEAKING YOUR TRUTH Ajoite, aquamarine, blue opal, bronzite, covellite, dumortierite, goshenite, **indicolite** kyanite, petalite, and **turquoise** encourage authenticity and living life according to your own spirituality.

STRENGTH Carry or wear abalone shell, anhydrite, hematite, **rutilated quartz**, or sunstone when you need extra physical strength (good for sportspeople).

TEAMWORK (IN SPORT, BUSINESS OR ANY GROUP) Fluorite, herderite, jadeite, sandstone, sodalite, spirit quartz, tourmaline, **yellow fluorite**, and zincite promote teamwork.

TIME MANAGEMENT Morganite and **staurolite** help you organize your time effectively.

TRAVEL A journey can be a walk to the corner shop, a trip round the world or following your path through life. Whatever your journey, **aquamarine**, cleavelandite, moonstone, schalenblende, reversed watermelon tourmaline, **turquoise**, and yellow jasper keep you safe.

WELLBEING Blue quartz gives you a general sense of health and happiness.

ZEST FOR LIFE Quartz crystal boosts your enthusiasm and helps you live life to the full.

Glossary

Absent healing The process of sending healing energy, good thoughts or prayers to a person who is not present – perhaps someone in another country. Also known as distant healing.

Akashic records A library of spiritual information that exists on another plane.

Asterism An optical effect that results in a star-like appearance.

Astigmatism A visual defect caused by the unequal curving of one or more of the refractive surfaces of the eye, usually the cornea.

Astral projection The ability to consciously send a part of the astral/spirit body outside the physical body to a specific location (while remaining connected to the physical body).

Astral travel The ability to send a part of the astral/spirit body to travel outside the physical body (while remaining connected to the physical body).

ADD Attention deficit disorder.

ADHA Attention deficit hyperactivity (disorder)

ADHD Attention deficit hyperactivity disorder.

Aura The energy field around the body.

Blade Describes a crystal that resembles a flat knife blade.

Botryoidal Describes bulbous minerals that resemble a bunch of grapes in appearance.

Chakra The Sanskrit word for "wheel". Chakras are the energy centers of the body (they appear as wheels to people who see energy). The correct use is "chakrum" (singular) and "chakra" (plural), but "chakra" and "chakras" are so widely used that I have stayed with this form throughout the book.

Channeling The communication of messages or information from the spirit world via a medium.

Chatoyancy An optical effect, also known as "cat's eye", found in different polished crystals. Cat's eye crystals bring good luck, happiness, and serenity. They raise intuition, awareness, and protection and can help with

disorders of the eyes, night vision, and headaches. The astrological associations of cat's eye crystals are Capricorn, Taurus, and Aries.

Chi In Chinese medicine and philosophy, chi is the energy or life force of the universe, believed to flow round the body and to be present in all living things. Other cultures call chi by different names. For example, ki (Japan) and prana (India).

Clairaudience The ability to hear psychic information.

Clairsentience The ability to sense psychic energies.

Clairvoyance The ability to see psychic information.

Dendrite A mineral that crystallizes in the shape of a tree or branch, or grows through another crystal or rock creating the impression of a tree or branches.

Dis-ease A state of unsoundness on any level (physical, emotional, mental, or spiritual) that may weaken the body's natural defence systems and increase the risk of illness or disease. It relates to underlying causes and not a specific illness or disease. **Distant healing** See **Absent healing**

Diverticulitis An infection of diverticula (abnormal protrusions in the gut).

Dodecahedral A solid figure with 12 equal pentagonal faces meeting in threes at 20 apexes.

Druse A surface crust of small crystals on a rock of the same or a different mineral.

Energy A supply or source of power: electrical, nuclear, mechanical, or subtle, such as chi.

Feldspar A group of silicate minerals.

Fire See **Iridescence**

Flow The Taoist concept of allowing things to happen naturally. When you follow your true path in life, things happen easily, as if you are floating along a stream. When you diverge from your path, things are harder to achieve and, eventually, you are stopped in your tracks by events or illness.

Geopathic stress Energy that emanates from the earth and is detrimental to human health. Two sources of this energy may be underground moving water or radiation from cell phone masts. Geopathic stress is linked with a long list of ailments, ranging from headaches to cancer.

Hemeralopia Impaired vision in daylight (yet normal night vision).

Hypoglycemia An abnormally low level of sugar in the blood.

Inclusion A mineral found within the structure of a different mineral.

Iridescence Colors appearing inside a crystal due to either diffraction or refraction of light within the crystalline structure.

Mass Matter that has no definable crystalline structure.

Meridian An energy pathway through the body. Meridians carry chi in the same way that veins and arteries carry blood.

Octahedral Shaped like an octahedron (a solid with eight faces).

Orthorhombic A crystal system with three axes of different lengths that cross at right angles.

Oxidation A chemical reaction in which oxygen is added to an element or compound, often producing a rust-like appearance.

Piezoelectric effect The electric current produced by some crystals when they are subjected to mechanical pressure.

Piezoelectricity The transducer effect that is caused by applying pressure to a crystal. This allows the transmutation of electrical to mechanical energy. This creates a physical vibration which, in quartz crystal resonates at a regular and constant frequency. This effect is very stable. So, if you have a quartz watch – and the quartz crystal is pure and cut at the correct angle to its axis – it will be accurate.

Pleochroic A physical property in which certain crystals transmit different colors when viewed along different axes.

Pyroelectric effect The production of electric charges on opposite faces of some crystals caused by a change in temperature.

Pyroelectricity The movement of electrons that results in a migration of positive and negative charges to opposite ends of a crystal. Caused by temperature changes. This is clearly seen in many crystals, especially tourmaline and quartz crystals. A weak effect can be observed in any crystal that has a polar axis.

Plagioclase A series of feldspars, including labradorite and sunstone.

Pseudomorph A mineral that replaces another within the original's crystal structure. As a result, the new mineral has the external shape of the departed one.

Psychic abilities These include intuition or gut feelings, channeling, clairvoyance, clairaudience, clairsentience, sensing energies and auras, seeing auras, interpreting auras, telepathy, extra-sensory perception, telepathy, and increased insight into divination and tarot card readings.

Record keeper Describes a crystal with raised triangles on the face of the termination.

Reiki A form of hands-on healing that originated in Japan and now has millions of practitioners worldwide.

Remote viewing The ability to see places and events at a distance. See also **Astral travel**

Restless leg syndrome Cramps in the legs that interfere with sleep at night.

Rhombic Describes crystals with a parallelogram shape (a parallelogram has four equal sides and oblique angles).

Rhombododecahedral Describes crystals that have 12 equal sides with oblique angles.

Rhombohedral See **Rhombic**

Scalenohedral Describes crystals that have 12 faces, each with three unequal sides.

Shamanic healing One of the oldest forms of traditional healing.

Sphenoid Wedge-shaped.

Spirit guides The beings or energies of departed souls who impart information, knowledge, and wisdom to help you on your path.

Tabular Describes crystals that are broad and flat.

Tetrahedral Describes crystals that have four faces.

Trapezohedral Describes crystals that have trapezium-shaped faces.

Trapezium A quadrilateral with two parallel sides.

Totem animals Animal spirits or characteristics that help to guide you on your path in life.

Index

Main crystal entries are listed in **bold**. Please note that physical ailments are listed in alphabetical order on pages 106-23.

Acknowledgments

I would like to thank my wife Lyn Palmer for her unwavering love and support. Also my staff at the time of writing; all the people at CICO Books: Liz, Kesta, Jerry, Sally, and Nick who worked on the first edition, Carmel, for her help with the second edition, and particularly Cindy for the good sense to publish this book; the people who inspired me to write – my father Cyril, Cassandra Eason, Melody, all my clients and students; and Ian, who knows why.

My sincere thanks to every other crystal author, whether or not I've read their books, and everyone inspired to heal themselves or others through this book.

Philip Permutt's website is found at www.thecrystalhealer.co.uk.
You can also like Philip Permutt on Facebook and follow him on Twitter: @1CrystalHealer.